YOU SHOOK MY HAND

MY HAND

Once Upon a Wartime 12

Extracts from the Diary of
Sergeant William C. Rose R.A.F.V.R 917922.
Japanese P.O.W.

Dedicated to my beloved wife, Joyce
and in memory of those with whom I served

1912 - 2002

*This is a picture of Joyce aged 20
and the frame which I made and
carried with me in Japan
'My most treasured posession'*

YOU SHOOK
MY HAND

Extracts from the Diary of
Sergeant William C. Rose R.A.F.V.R 917922.
Japanese P.O.W.

Once Upon a Wartime 12

Acknowledgements

I would like to express my sincere thanks to:

Malcolm and Lindy, Robyn, Graham and Takako and Jonathan for encouraging and assisting in producing the printed sheets from my hand-written diary entries and placing them on to computer disks.

&

To Derek R Peachey for his substantial research and co-authorship for my fuller historical version *(Details on page 136).*

First Published in Great Britain in 2002 by
Barny Books

The Original Diaries are held at the
Imperial War Museum, London, UK

Published by Barny Books, Hough on the Hill, Grantham, Lincolnshire
Produced by: TUCANN*design&print*, 19 High Street, Heighington Lincoln LN4 1RG
Tel & Fax: 01522 790009
www.tucann.co.uk

Contents

Chapter One
Early Days

I was born in Bermondsey, London in 1912. It was an industrial area that principally manufactured glue, scent and leatherwork. I went to the local elementary school and left when I was fourteen. My father had fought in the First World War and suffered from the effects of gassing at the front, but he had managed to get a job as a port wine blender and I went and worked with him for a few months when I left school.

My cousin Ernest said that he could get me a permanent job with his firm and this he did. Ernest had served in the R.H.A. during the war, (The Royal Horse Artillery), driving horses to deliver the ammunition to the guns at the front. As a result of this, he had managed to get a job as Transport Manager for Robert Adlard and Co, a firm of roof tilers. Transport was all by horse and cart in those days.

My job was in the office, filing and maintaining the company records. I worked there for a few months, then I was transferred to work at the weighbridge on the company's wharf. It was fitted with an English five ton crane and a ten ton Dutch one. The company imported tiles and bricks from Holland, slates from Wales and cement from Belgium. My job was to keep details of all these materials. These were all carried by barge. Two years later, the firm opened a branch at Wood Green and I was given the job of managing the materials that arrived by rail. It was a good opportunity and I had to think of my own future so I started attending evening classes in book keeping and business economics as well as seminars on building materials. I had to manage the unloading, stacking, recording and releasing the materials and, at nineteen, I was pleased with the success I was making in the firm.

Everything was working out well until Ernest Taylor, the brother of the Company Secretary, joined the branch. He started issuing me with orders and that didn't go down well. I didn't like his attitude and I didn't attempt to hide my resentment. After a while the Company Chairman summoned me to the head office to explain myself. I explained how I felt. He offered me the choice of either moving to a branch in Essex or Kent. I chose Kent and started work at Strood near Rochester. I lived with my parents and went to work by train. I was working at a small roofing depot under the management of Robert Shales. We got on really well and he taught me a lot about the business, so much so that I was offered the job of setting up a new branch across the river at Rochester. The future looked bright despite the Spanish Civil War raging in Europe and the rise of the Third Reich in Germany. I moved into digs in Chatham and asked my childhood sweetheart to become my wife.

Joyce Heather Khan and I had met at Church, St. Lawrence Jewry, Guildhall, in 1926. I had been a chorister and, later on, a bell ringer. Joyce's

grandfather had been an Afghan and Persian Ambassador to Russia where he had been murdered during the political troubles. Her father had attended school in England and been in the Medical Corps in the Boer War. When he returned, he had married Joyce's mother who was known as Dickie. Ten years later, Joyce had been born. She was born a month and a half before me and I always told them that they were saving their daughter for me to arrive.

We returned to the Church where we had met to be married. We had built a bungalow in Robin Hood Lane at the top of Bluebell Hill. It was an idyllic spot to start our married life. The lane went through a chestnut wood which was carpeted with bluebells in the

'Corpie' my father in law, son of an Afghan diplomat and Hallkeeper at Gresham College in the City of London from 1918 to 1942

spring. It was a beautiful, peaceful spot. Unfortunately, the bliss of those prewar days was suddenly cut short. I received a letter from the Company Secretary saying that they were reducing the number of employees. I was out of a job. It wasn't easy to find work in prewar days.

There had been a lot of unemployment and poverty between the wars. I registered for military service and was placed on the deferred list. I signed up with the Auxiliary Fire Service while I was waiting to hear from them. Five months later, I was summoned to report to R.A.F. Uxbridge for basic training. I was in the Royal Air Force Voluntary Reserve.

We had already begun to experience the consequences of war. Blackout was enforced. It was quite eerie walking down our lane at night without a glimmer of light to guide us. Shortages were beginning to appear. Sugar, meat and butter were the first foods to be rationed and now, after two years of marriage, I had to leave my beloved Joyce and report for training.

Mother-in-law 'Dickie' the indomitable - a mother-in-law in a million who was loved by all the family

I was kitted out at Uxbridge and then reported to Blackpool for initial training. We marched, we did square bashing, we did fitness training, we did musketry practice. We became proficient and fit. I was then posted to Wattisham, a newly built Blenheim bomber station and aerodrome in Suffolk. I was drafted into the Station Defence Section and promoted to corporal. Then, with similar haste, I was promoted to sergeant because of the many bombing casualties and put in charge of the Station Defence Office. Among my other newly aquired duties I was required to train young cadets in drill movements. It was all very interesting despite the fact that the station was bombed nineteen times while I was there. It was a very different life to that of being a civilian.

In July of 1941, I was suddenly sent to a gunnery school on the Isle of Man. I had hardly started the training when I was recalled to Wattisham for overseas posting. The thought of going abroad came as a shock, particularly as we were only given three days embarkation notice. I could only think of Joyce and the thought of leaving her. She had never been far from my mind. Now my feelings became more intense but we had to

9

917922 Aircraftsman Second Class (AC2)
William Cyril Rose RAFVR, taken at Blackpool
in June 1940 to give to my Joyce
and the 1940 photograph of my
lovely wife Joyce - a photograph
that never left me in my travels
throughout the 'war'

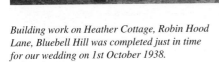

Building work on Heather Cottage, Robin Hood
Lane, Bluebell Hill was completed just in time
for our wedding on 1st October 1938.

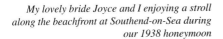

My lovely bride Joyce and I enjoying a stroll
along the beachfront at Southend-on-Sea during
our 1938 honeymoon

make the most of the few hours we had left together. Joyce had a job working for Kent County Council so I knew she would be able to manage and, as it happened, a friend came to stay with her while I was away so she wouldn't be completely on her own. We had also had the foresight to build a cottage for Joyce's mother further along Robin Hood Lane. I knew in my heart of hearts that she would be alright but it didn't make parting any easier. We didn't know when we would see each other again and there was always the possibility that I would not be coming home, but we thrust those thoughts to the back of our minds and enjoyed our last few days together.

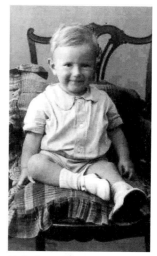

Malcolm, our first born at 14 months of age. The photograph was taken in July 1943 during a visit to my family in Catford, London, by Joyce and Malcolm

Our boss, my fellow NCOs and myself (arrowed) pictured at a sports day at RAF Wattisham, Suffolk in 1941. Notice we are carrying the mandatory gas masks, as was required at all times

11

The lads of RAF Wattisham, Suffolk, 'making hay while the sun shone' at a base Christmas Party in 1941. I am on the left (Circled).

Chapter Two
Reporting for Duty

I reported to West Kirby Liverpool where we were issued with tropical gear. Nobody would tell us where we were going and we had quite convinced ourselves that we were set for the Middle East. We embarked on a splendid new liner, the RMS Andes of some 25,000 tons. It hadn't even completed its maiden voyage. We were its first passengers. We couldn't believe our luck and we soon settled down to life aboard, not that we went very far. The ship remained in Liverpool Docks. The war seemed to be a long way away even though the Battle of Britain was raging in Southern England and I often wondered how Joyce was coping back in Robin Hood Lane. Liverpool Docks were fine but, at the end of November, we moved out to join a convoy in the Irish Sea. That was a different matter. A lot of the men failed to turn up for breakfast in the morning and I began to feel very unwell myself. The sight of a hard boiled egg was more than I could bear. I don't recall much of the next few days but, as a

The RMS Andes, Flagship of the Royal Mail Lines Ltd, was built by Harland and Wolff Ltd, Belfast. The ship's characteristics were: Weight 25,676 tons; Length 669.25 feet; Depth 47.5 feet; Service Speed 21 knots; Passengers - 1st Class 324, 2nd Class 204; Twin screw turbines and was in service between the United Kingdom and South America.

A pencilled sketch of Table Mountain, South Africa, from the deck of RMS Andes as we arrived in Table Bay, Cape Town on 5th January 1942, "...before rounding the Cape

South Beach, Durban

Ship entering Durban Harbour

sergeant, I hardly think I set a good example. I couldn't ever remember feeling so ill in my life and I wasn't the only one to suffer. I had always thought of seasickness as a joke but not any more after that experience. Fortunately the sickness did wear off and I was able to face the shipboard meals again.

Once the Andes had joined the convoy, we sailed into the Atlantic. Life on board was pleasant. We had exercise periods as well as machine gun stripping and military drills. The only real concern was of the German U boats that were known to be patrolling the area. We were sailing through the submarine infested waters of the Atlantic. The ships in the convoy zig-zagged through the seas attempting to avoid them. On the 21st of December, we arrived off Sierra Leone in West Africa. It was a wonderful sight. Seeing green clad coasts again and smelling the lush aroma of tropical fruits and feeling the warmth of the sun on our skins did wonders to our morale. Bumboats surrounded the ship and native boys dived for coins that we threw into the water. They offered us fruit to buy but first it had to be soaked in permanganate of potash to

14

disinfect it.

We spent Christmas Day there with a proper Christmas dinner even though the heat was almost unbearable. I took time off to think of Joyce and my family back at home. Joyce was expecting our first child and, although it was a happy day with the men, I wished I could have had it with her.

We set sail again on Boxing Day, completely oblivious of what was happening in the rest of the world. We passed Table Mountain and Lion Head on our way to Table Bay at Cape Town, where we anchored. I could only wonder at the sights and experiences that were coming my way. These were things I had only read about and now I was seeing them for real. There were so many things that I wished my Joycie could have shared with me, the Ceremony of Crossing the Line when we reached the Equator, the 'bumboat' boys surrounding the ship at Sierra Leone like bees round a honey pot, the deep verdant green of the coast line and the smell of the vegetation and the grandeur of Table Mountain. Then we sailed on to Durban where we arrived on January the 10th. We were allowed ashore there and we met with such hospitality from the South African people that it took any thought of war completely out of our minds. I met up with the wonderful Rein family and they took me to their home. The whole area was coloured by flowering shrubs and trees. We talked and ate luscious fruit. They were good, kind people and their hospitality was something I have never forgotten. They promised to write to my family when I returned to my ship and they did. They also sent Joyce a wonderful parcel but, of course, it was years later that I heard about that.

We were transferred to the S.S. City of Canterbury, a much older ship that had been used to transport Italian Prisoners of War. It was in a disgusting state. It was infested with cockroaches and the sleeping quarters were atrocious. The conditions were so bad that five hundred of the troops walked off before we sailed. Three hundred did return but the rest were left parading on the dockside when we set sail. We never did discover what happened to them. As we moved out of the docks, whistles of the trains on the dockside and of the other ships alongside filled the air repeating the morse code for V - dot, dot, dot, dash - the V for Victory. When the pilot left us, he stood to attention and saluted us. We gave him a cheer, but he was soon a dot on the horizon disappearing into the mist that hid South Africa from us, a wonderful country and wonderful people.

Chapter Three
Trouble at Sea

The S.S. City of Canterbury had 1,053 servicemen on board, 850 of which were members of the R.A.F. The crew was mainly Lascar. We were kept busy on the voyage, mainly getting the ship clean. We weren't ordered to scrub the decks, but were pleased to do it, if only to get better conditions on board. Then we had our other duties and drills and a series of lectures about life in the Far East. We had four Bofors guns mounted on deck and one 12 pounder AA gun. We also had 27 light machine guns and 2 systems of Pyrotecnics and Cables. We sailed in a convoy of 21 ships, half of which went on to Aden. We were told that we would be sailing to Bombay but a change of orders kept us sailing on. By this time our normal food stocks had run out and we had to use the reserve stocks. The water was horrible, always warm. This was when the captain told us that Hong Kong had surrendered and so we were diverting to Singapore. It was then mid January and Hong Kong had surrendered on December 25th. The news blackout had certainly been effective.

Our section of the convoy took passage through the Sunda Strait between Sumatra and Java when nine Japanese aircraft attacked. The noise as they swept down towards us was startling. Fortunately none of the bombs they dropped did any damage to us or either of the other two ships that were sailing with us, the Felix Roustel and The Empress of Asia but it warned us how close we were to the enemy. The voyage had been uneventful until that moment. I think we all felt apprehensive.

Our escorting cruiser, HMS Dunera, had signalled for us to act independently and we had moved away from the other two troop ships when the next wave of Japanese planes came in. Some of the men were sunbathing on the deck when one of them pointed up at the sky and said, "Look at that," and there were the dive bombers coming in at us. They came from all directions, eighteen of them in all. We saw them before we heard them. The noise as they approached grew louder until it became a roar and drowned out all other sounds. They approached the City of Canterbury at

The City of Canterbury in the lagoon in Venice in 1946. She was then transporting displaced persons - Polish and Austrian Jews - from Port Said to Trieste and Venice.

full speed, dropping their bombs all round us and shooting up the decks before they lifted and came in again. We shot at them with everything we had but it didn't seem to stop them coming at us again and again. We were steaming full ahead during the attack with the helmsman swinging the ship from side to side to avoid the bombs. Then a bomb exploded by the starboard beam, severing the telemoter pipes which put the steering gear out of action. We were swept towards the Felix Roustel which was in a similar position to ourselves, unable to steer. We could see them fighting fires on their deck but somehow we avoided a collision. The ship had to be stopped to prevent it driving ashore and for seven minutes we were sitting ducks. But in that seven minutes the engineers had changed to the after steering position and we managed to continue under way. As we broke free, so nine more Japanese bombers came screaming in. One of the bombs was a near miss. I saw the three copper bands on it as it fell into the sea alongside us but it failed to go off. We were running out of ammunition, especially for the Bofors. Medical orderlies were busy dealing with the wounded and everywhere was hidden by smoke and we were deafened by the constant noise. Then, at 1145 we passed N°. 1 beacon and the attack petered out. We had been under continuous attack for an hour and a half and it felt like for ever. Both the Empress of Asia and the Felix Roustel had been seriously damaged. A Free French ship was on fire and the men had had to abandon ship. We had seen the naval and many local boats going in to rescue them as we passed into the Singapore Roads.

Captain Percival RNR was awarded the OBE. It was only his skill that saved us from being sunk.

As we approached the harbour, a naval launch came alongside and an officer shouted at us through a megaphone, "What the bloody hell are you doing here?" What a welcome...

Singapore was covered in a pall of smoke and there were sounds of explosions and guns firing. The docksides were stacked with supplies and abandoned cars which people who had managed to get passage away from the island had left. Warehouses had been bombed or were burning, yet life was still going on. Ships were being unloaded. People were arriving and lorries leaving. As soon as a Japanese plane appeared overhead, the local labour force disappeared and the servicemen were left to unload their own ships. The whole place was teeming with troops and equipment.

Our own officer's priority was to arrange to bury the three men that had been killed in the air attack. We stood to attention as the three coffins were taken off the ship, Harry Brewster, a married man with three children from the East End of London; Bert Shaw, one of the soldiers and a Lascar seaman. Then the wounded were collected by launch and taken to the hospital in Singapore. The soldiers were the next to leave after their equipment had been unloaded. The R.A.F. personnel stayed on board and that evening, the City of Canterbury set sail for Batavia in Java.

The leafy environs of the King William III School, Batavia, where we enjoyed a much needed rest after disembarking from the City of Canterbury and before marching off to the Dutch Barracks at Buitenzorg

Our arrival in Java seemed to cause the authorities some concern. They hadn't expected us and they didn't know what to do with us. They hadn't been ready for the sudden turn of events at Singapore and they certainly weren't prepared for another batch of troops. I have no idea what fortunes befell The Empire Star which had also set sail for Batavia at the same time as we did. We settled down in the King William III School and made ourselves comfortable but

18

we weren't there for long. We had to make our way to the Dutch barracks at Buitenzorg on foot. Our kit and equipment followed slowly behind us in Thorneycroft lorries that we had acquired at the dockside. Our time at the barracks was spent doing the occasional guard duty, keeping an eye on the ammunition trucks and generally lounging around but our days there were cut short. With the fall of Singapore, it was obvious that we needed to put as much distance as possible between ourselves and any Japanese invasion. So we set off again in the same order. We were on foot and the lorries, loaded with our kit, trundled along behind us. We were making our way to Tjilatjap some 150 miles from Buitenzorg. It was exhausting. It was a mountainous area and the weather was hot, sticky and damp. We stopped at Soekaboemi that first night, the night of March 4th, on the

southern side of the first mountain range we had crossed. All I wanted to do was to sink on to the ground and sleep but I quickly returned to the land of the living when I was shaken awake and told I was to detail the guards for the night: a rather difficult task in the dark duty that night.

The temple in the Governor's palace grounds of Buitenzorg. The grounds were particularly picturesque.

We set off again early the next morning in the same order but, fortunately, the walkers were some way ahead of the lorries. A squadron of Japanese fighters flew in over the convoy and shot up the lorries but they weren't good shots. There was no damage.

We arrived at Garoet early on the morning of March 6th but were only allowed a short rest before we left again for Tjilatjap. This was even more arduous. The mountains through which we had to go were steeper and more forbidding than before. But with all that foot slogging, we thought we were getting well away from the Japanese. Those hopes were soon dashed. On March 8th, we were told that the Dutch had capitulated. We'd had very little to do with the Dutch to that point and we began regretting leaving so much equipment back at the docks, especially the gun barrels.

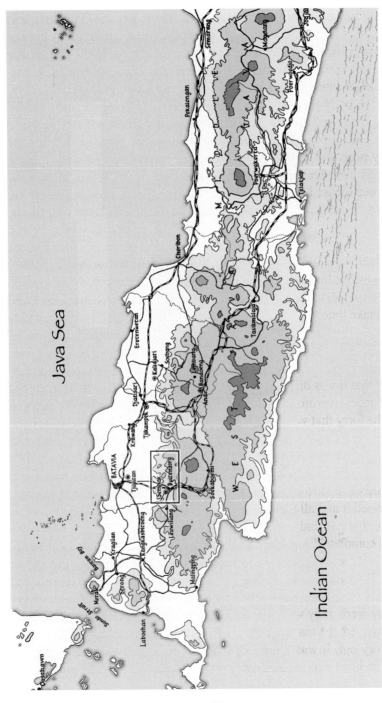

The island of Java, showing the names of its cities and towns before the Second World War. Semplak (in box) was due South of Batavia (now known as Djarkata, or Jarkata). As can be seen, compared to Tjilatjap, Semplak was barely a stone's throw (almost) from Buitenzorg. We could have saved ourselves a lot of trekking if we'd known what we were to know later.

20

We continued our trek through the mountains when the C.O. called us together and told us that we were now surrounded by Japanese forces and, as a consequence, 'Colonel Black's Force' as we were known, were now Prisoners of War. And we hadn't fired one shot in anger! Neither had we seen a single Japanese soldier in Java and Singapore - only their aircraft and bombs and gunfire.

He followed this up by telling us that we had to stack all our weapons and stay where we were and await developments. None of us were particularly perturbed at this stage. We were pleased to settle down and get some well earned rest. Then we started sorting out our kit so that we could lighten our loads. This was particularly difficult for me. I had loaded so much personal kit and I didn't want to give up any of it. The rest of the day was very confused. We weren't sure what was going to happen or what to expect. We spent the night in a Javanese village in bamboo huts built on stilts. Then we resumed our march, making for a tea plantation about seven miles away but first of all, we got rid of any military equipment that could have been of use to the Japs. We sent it rolling down the mountainside and it didn't take long to destroy the whole lot. Machine guns and ammunition lorries and fuel, all of it brand new, everything was destroyed. Then we set off again. It was a nightmare. It rained and rained as it can only rain in tropical countries. The mountains were so steep and the paths became so slippery that it was difficult to keep our balance. It was so bad that one of our kit lorries overturned and completely blocked the road and, of course, it was the lorry that was carrying mine! It all had to be unloaded. I had to make an on the spot decision, which kit bag to keep. The most difficult thing for me to decide was which books I wanted to keep. I didn't want to toss any of them away but the Good Lord took a hand in the proceedings and made the decision for me. Another lorry ran over one of my kitbags and crushed it and all the contents into the deep, rutted mud.

Torrential rain and yet more rain continued to fall without pause. It was a day of complete discomfort, frustration and mud. The locals sold us cups of tea without sugar or milk and we managed to buy fruit from them, some of which we had never seen before: sour jack which was like a grapefruit and paw-paws, ramboetangs, which had a hard skin and zurzaks. Whatever they were, they were all most welcome.

We arrived at a tea plantation on March 12th and at long last, we were able to dry out. It was a general assembly point and we were more than pleased to be met by a bunch of Australians who had got themselves well settled in. They quickly brewed us some tea and cooked us some rice. Pilot Officer Bird, who had bought and cooked a lamb, treated a few of us, who had gathered in a hut, to a right royal meal. It was served with army rations and potatoes and it was superb.

We settled in at the tea plantation but on March 20th, we were loaded on to lorries and taken to a market place called Wonaragi. The lorries were driven by Aussies and they drove like lunatics. It was the most hair raising journey I have ever had and we were all pleased to climb out in one piece. That was when we saw our first Jap soldiers and where we were informed that we were to march to Batavia some 280 miles away at 23 miles a day. They had to be joking but, in case they weren't, we set to on a massive shoe repairing and purchase campaign.

The next day, that order was countermanded. We were assembled and marched to Garoel Station on March 21st. From there, we continued to Semplak Aerodrome, arriving at night on March 26th. We were allocated billets and spent the next few nights settling in and making ourselves comfortable. Our billet was a Javanese hotel, a sizeable, single storey building built mainly of bamboo and atup. It was on the perimeter of the airfield. A water supply was organised and we were able to have wonderful, cold showers using four gallon oil cans or standing in front of a burst cold water supply pipe gushing at full pressure. It was here that the Japanese began to make us realise the privileged position they had over us.

We were roused at 0600 hours and lined up for Tenko (roll call) at 0610 hours. Breakfast was from 0645 hours to 0730. We were expected to work from 0800 hours to 1100 and from 1230 until 1630. Tenko was repeated at 1730 and lights out were at 1930.

We were to be allowed to write one letter a month which would be censored. Our name, rank, number and service had to be included. When our senior officer, Wing Commander G.F. Alexander refused to give certain details or to work, he earned himself a slapping in front of all the troops, confined in Japanese quarters for two weeks and relieved of his command. From then on Wing Commander Matthews became the senior officer of Colonel Black's Force.

The whole camp abounded with rumours. They weren't very accurate but they did a lot to boost morale and gave us a lot to dream about. They soon got to be known as 'duffgen'. I was assigned to a work party that was filling in holes on the airfield. It was tough physical work in the hot humid climate but we had a few days respite when the steamroller fell into one of the bomb craters. Leisure activities were organised in the camp to try and maintain morale. There were football matches, poetry readings, Malay lessons, community singing and morning and evening services. Flying Officer Bevan conducted the services. He held a service on Sunday, April 5th to celebrate Easter. The Japanese did not understand our religion but we did not have to work for the rest of the day and the following morning, each man was issued with a rare, small loaf. Later that day, the first Japanese planes landed at the airfield.

I busied myself in my spare time. I had been able to obtain materials from a vacant building site. Some of the men made rings and ornaments from the materials they found and they became sought after. I made drawing equipment from the perspex from broken aircraft windows and sandals from an old tyre. I made board games, bagatelle and draughts and musical instruments. I used the resin from local trees as gum. I didn't waste a thing. My most ambitious effort was to make a keyboard for a chap called Williams. He had been a pianist on B.B.C. radio. The strings were to be various strands of aerial wire. The keyboard range was $5^1/_2$ octaves. I used teak for the main keys and balsa for the black ones. The strings were to be held in position with screws across a teak frame. 'Tojo', the camp Commandant was very interested in this piano after he had first slapped me because I hadn't saluted him quickly enough. He had come up behind me and I hadn't seen him. He made up for it though by allowing me to use an outbuilding for a workshop. By and large our life there was bearable but there were two drawbacks, the food and health. Our diet was soup and rice and that did not satisfy us, We were always hungry and it wasn't long before I had to adjust my trousers. I had lost so much weight, that they were too big for me. General health on the camp was causing concern. Mosquitoes were a permanent problem. Uncovered cesspits were treated with kerosene and we were inoculated twice because of the increase in sickness - 1,500 cases out of the 4,000 men in the camp. Ringworm was common. Zambuk and iodine helped to deal with that and, fortunately, I managed to get mine under control within five days but I was badly affected by heat rash which was at its worst when I showered. I also had bad stomach aches and a sore toe. I had dropped a hammer on it! A rice poultice dealt with that. Depression became a common occurrence and crutch irritation was a general problem. We finally received an issue of soap and that helped.

We had plenty of books on the camp. I always had enjoyed reading but, one evening, Lofty decided that books were not enough. He was going to tell us all a bed time story. Lofty was one of the characters that a situation, such as we had found ourselves in, throws up. He gave us a witty and uplifting version of 'Death Valley' and, from then on, his story telling became a nightly request. Lofty was involved with spreading of the "duffgen" but he did it in such a conspiratorial manner that we couldn't take offence even when the information was outrageous. He kept the source of his information a tight secret.

Then the locals stopped accepting the Japanese paper money (invasion money). So the Japs refused to let any more food or fruit be passed over the fence to us and they closed off the roads around the camp. That was a big loss because we had relied on this food to implement the poor diet. Then some of our officers forgot to salute the guards at the gate and that brought serious trouble. It generated an epidemic of bashing. Not only were the officers bashed, so was everyone else. In addition to that, our rations were cut. Health problems were always with us. I had another attack of the dreaded ringworm. Fortunately I had enough ointment to deal with it myself. But then I caught a cold and I couldn't shake it off. I began to feel lethargic and depressed and the 'duffgen' circulating round the camp didn't do anything to lift my spirits.

We had a new 'Tojo' in May. He was quite a decent chap as long as he wasn't provoked so we were very careful how we spoke to him. He surprised us one day by supplying those of us who were working on the airfield with tea. That was the day I managed to win a trip out of the camp on a lorry to collect gravel. It was also the day I discovered the ringworm had appeared on my right knee yet again. But, at last, my cold was getting better. Instead of the usual watery soup and rice, we had stew for dinner that night. It was surprising how much better a single meal could make us feel. I returned to my self imposed task of building a brick path to the latrines. The lads took hand barrows out of the camp to collect more bricks for the next stage of the path. It so happened that outside the perimeter of the camp there was a partially built bungalow with various building materials scattered about...bricks, doors, teak, balsa wood, screws etc a lucky find for me. It was a good job they did because the following morning we were told that they would no longer be able to continue taking the barrows out. We weren't given any reason for the decision but the Japs were good at suddenly producing these rules without reason. It was this week that the Australian nurses were taken out of the camp and replaced with Eura

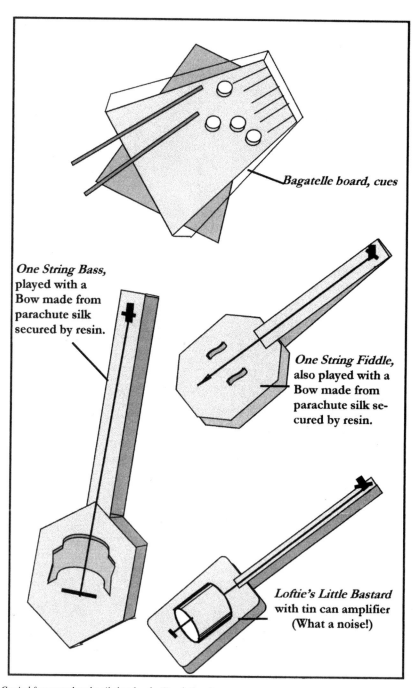

Bagatelle board, cues

One String Bass, played with a Bow made from parachute silk secured by resin.

One String Fiddle, also played with a Bow made from parachute silk secured by resin.

Loftie's Little Bastard with tin can amplifier (What a noise!)

Copied from my thumbnail sketches by Derek Peachey

25

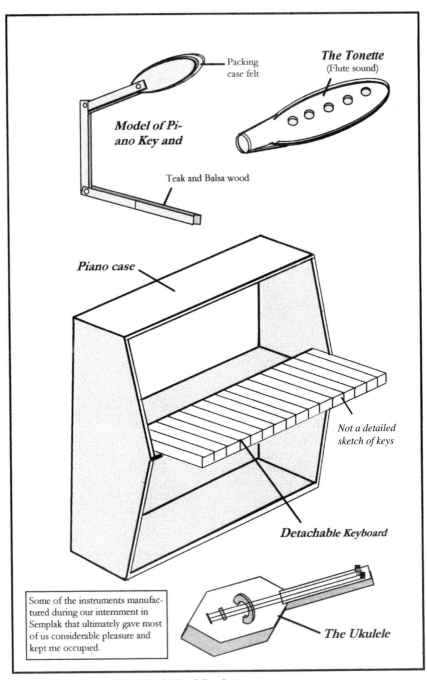

Packing case felt

The Tonette
(Flute sound)

*Model of Pi-
ano Key and*

Teak and Balsa wood

Piano case

*Not a detailed
sketch of keys*

Detachable Keyboard

Some of the instruments manufactured during our internment in
Semplak that ultimately gave most
of us considerable pleasure and
kept me occupied.

The Ukulele

Copied from my thumbnail sketches by Derek Peachey

sian ones. Once again, no explanation was given.

New guards arrived that week and 'Tojo' took the opportunity to familiarise us with a few more 'Nip' commands such as Kiwotuke (attention), Yasomi (stand at ease), Migi Muke (right turn) and Hidari Muke (left turn). We had to keep practising these until 'Tojo' was pleased with our progress.

May 14th and anti aircraft fire was heard coming from the west of the camp and loud explosions were heard. The following morning, we were informed that our vegetable allowance was to be halved. We wondered what was happening and it didn't take long for the 'duffgen' to kick into action. The news all seemed good. We heard that the Americans were bombing Japanese positions and that the Japs were retreating. We quite convinced ourselves that we would be home for Christmas and Lofty insisted that he was going to get me hopelessly drunk and return me to my wife in person. May gave way to June and then to July but the parole we had been promised failed to materialise. We still reported for work on the aerodrome but there was little for us to do and we would often return to the camp early. Football matches were held daily. There were concerts and lectures but the days became boring. It was only the thought of parole that kept us all cheerful. There were several incidents that lightened the time. We all stopped to watch a Javanese wedding procession going by the camp. It was preceded by a band that played the Woodpecker song. Another time the Jap guards turned on one of the local staff and beat him up. It turned out that he had stolen a watch. But mostly it was waiting, waiting for the day that we would go home and there wasn't a day went by that I didn't think of Joyce and my family back in England.

August 1st and we were still at Semplak. 'duffgen' and rumours still circulated but there was still no sign of parole. There was little to do so I carried on working on the piano that I was making. We had an all star concert that evening and it was good and certainly helped relieve our feelings of disappointment at not moving out. Sunday was much the same except for Church services morning and evening. I spent Monday completing the piano keys, all five and a half octaves and making specimen sections of the string movement using felt from a packing case.

I completed the frame on the 4th as the 'duffgen' started again. The rumour this time was that we were all being moved to Batavia. The Japs had sent all their oil stocks to the port. The Aussie drivers of the petrol lorries still wore their hair long and we wondered how they did it. Our heads were kept shorn and I was one of the barbers.

I finished the piano in time for my birthday on the 8th, a memorable day because that was when the orchestra performed in public for the first time. It comprised ukes, guitars, flute, a tin box covered with a gas cape to act as a drum, a string fiddle, a cello and a zonophone.

We had our usual Church services on the 9th and I celebrated my birthday a day late with a meal of egg and chips - sweet potatoes-, which I shared with Lofty and Williams, great. It was also the day that 'Tojo' had a photograph taken of all the allied officers with himself in the middle. He was a strange man.

It was a strange time. We knew something was going to happen but we didn't know what although "duffgen" was circulating even more quickly and, although we couldn't be sure of its veracity, it gave us hope. Then on Saturday, August 15th, whilst I was working on the piano frame and a football match was in progress, our officers were informed that we were to be ready to move at 0830 hours the next morning. The Japs always seemed to like action on a Sunday.

General upheaval and bedlam set in straight away with men sorting out their kit, throwing away the rubbish and retaining anything that might be useful. I decided my own kit could wait and set about dismantling the piano and packing it into sections that could be easily transported. What a night!

We were roused at 0630 hours the next morning, had breakfast at 0730 and walked out of Semplak at 0830 hours. Our heavy kit was carried by lorry and I left strict instructions with the transport officer on how my piano pack had to be handled. Then we started the walk to the station, some eight kilometres away. We travelled to Batavia by train where our numbers were checked and rechecked. Then we were marched to our new camp, Makasuru Camp, Camp N° 5, 11 kilometres away. The day was exceptionally hot and we were only allowed short rest periods. We had to keep moving. Some Dutch women threw tins of milk, cigarettes and chocolates to us when the guards weren't looking, bless them. They would have been punished if they had been seen. I can't tell you how much this meant to us because we had very little to eat or drink that day. Some of the men couldn't keep up and they dropped out of the line. They were picked up by the lorries.

The huts at the camp were typical of that region and built of bamboo, atup and bursam. They were set between rows of coconut trees. The officers were housed with the men at this camp. We only expected to be there overnight or a few days at the most but the long march must have dulled our reasoning. We should have realised that things moved very slowly in that part of the world.

I slept well that night although I was so hungry and the food we had next day wasn't enough to assuage our hunger, a ladle of rice at each meal, no soup, no vegetables, nothing to give us the nutrition we needed. The Japs did give us ten cigars per man each week though.

That evening we were joined by 150 Singapore Technical Corps (S.T.C.) lads, Chinese, Indians and Malaysians who had been in service with the R.A.F. in Singapore. Later on that day 500 other R.A.F. personnel came into the camp.

We had become settled at Sempak and we didn't feel like getting started on other activities. Besides anything else, my piano hadn't been brought on any of the lorries. The Wing Commander said he would have it brought up later but it still didn't come. 'Tojo' came and visited the camp and I stopped him and asked if he would arrange for the piano to be sent on but he said it was no concern of his and that was that. I didn't feel like starting anything else. I felt depressed. I think most of us did. The 'duffgen' had lead us to believe that we were going to be repatriated. The last rumour had been that we were going to be sent to Canada in exchange for Japanese P.O.W.s and we had believed it because we had wanted to believe it but I think we all realised that, as time went on, this was becoming more and more unlikely. 'duffgen' continued to circulate. The Yanks were recapturing Japanese held islands. The Germans were in full retreat. The technical corps boys managed to fix up a radio and we began to get some real news at last. It was the first time we knew for fact what was going on outside the camp.

The camp was run by four R.A.F. officers, Wing Commanders Alexander, King, Matthews and Fru. They organised concerts and keep fit sessions. They were enjoyable but I found it difficult to shake off this feeling of lethargy and depression. There wasn't a day went by that I didn't think of my Joyce back at home and our child that she was expecting.

It was while we were at Makasuru that we were ordered to sign an oath of obedience. None of us were prepared to sign such a thing but Wing Commander Alexander amended it to say that we were signing under duress and this is what we did.

Makasuru, Camp N° 5 was our home until October 18th when we were marched down to the docks in Batavia. We hadn't seen them since the day we had set off walking over the mountains and they did present a sad sight. The wreckage of ships jutted out from the waves but the worst sight was the Japanese flag flying.

Chapter Four
Journey to Japan as P.O.W.

W e embarked on a ship that can only be described as an old tub, the S.S. Singapore Maru. We were shunted into the ship's cargo hold which we were told was to be our accommodation to our destination. Japanese soldiers returning on leave had the centre part of the ship and a lot more room than we did. As soon as we sailed they started to sing in a monotonous, droning sound. It was dreadful, so we entertained them with some proper songs, British style. That helped our morale and we needed it. Fresh water was supplied for drinking only, one can per person per day. The only food we had was rice in a fish soup and you could detect a few tiddlers if you looked carefully. Queuing was the order of the day. We queued for everything. We queued for water and food and the latrines although that was only going over the side of the ship. The only good thing was the wonderful sunsets we saw.

In no time at all, the hold became smelly. It stank and there was no way we could get away from the smell. The decks grew greasier and greasier. I would close my eyes to shut it all out and it would be like living in a multicultural society, there was such a mixture of languages, Dutch, Javanese, Malayan, Indian, Chinese, Japanese and, of course, English.

It rained heavily during the voyage and it poured in through the open hatches. The Dutch had their sleeping bags under them but now they had to go and find a dry corner where they could stand. Fortunately our spaces remained fairly dry but those who were getting wet just had to put up with it. There was one good thing about the rain. It began to shift the grease that was congealing on the decks.

We arrived at Singapore on October 24th. We had been on that old tub for six days. We were told that we would march to Changi Prison Camp, a distance of fourteen miles, and carry our own kit. I looked round at the men around me. None of us were in a fit state to carry anything but there was no choice. We either carried it or it got left behind.

Our stay at Changi was only slightly less dismal than the voyage from

Java. We camped under canvas in heavy, torrential rain. There were no groundsheets and we had to balance on our kit bags to get some rest. We were only there for a few days. We walked back to the docks and embarked on yet another old tub, the SS Tokyo Maru.

It looked in even a worse state than the one that had brought us from Java if that was possible.

One hundred and eighty prisoners were packed into the lower hold. The deck was saturated with rain and we were told that the hatches had to be kept open. Humidity was high and, in no time at all, the hold began to smell. We stayed, interned in the hold for three days before the boat sailed. We actually moved out at 11 o'clock on October 30th. By then the smell in the hold was already revolting. There was little sleep that night. Heavy rain coming through the open hatch swamped everything in the overcrowded, unlit hold. There were no lights at all. Dysentery and beri-beri had already started to develop before we left Singapore and some of the men had had to be taken off the ship before we sailed. A lack of medical supplies meant there was little chance of being able to treat them. As light came, we took it in turns to shower beneath the open hatch but guess whose luck ran out when it was his turn. It stopped raining when I had stripped off and stood beneath the hole. It was as hot as hell in the hold and life quickly became intolerable and, to some, unbearable.

Our 'tub' was one of a convoy of five and I guess the conditions were the same on all of them. The word went round that we were heading for Saigon in Indo-China and we did arrive off the coast at 1000 hours on November 3rd. By that time, we didn't have the energy to create any incidents. We were almost in a state of limbo. The only thing we could do was to pray. I prayed. I prayed to be reunited with Joyce and our child, to be able to live a normal life again.

At last the boat was still so while we waited off Saigon, I resorted to some hair cutting to pass the time. The Japs wanted me to cut their hair as well and paid me with cigarettes. That helped some of the lads. They were really missing tobacco.

The next day, four of the ships sailed on while we went about forty miles up river where we presumed the boat was going to have some repair work done. Water was still unavailable, except for a small can to drink each day, so we had to remain dirty. By the November 5th, yellow fever and cholera had broken out and a cold that had started at Changi persisted so that I felt low in health as well as spirits. The sun was really hot and the boat had dropped anchor in a mangrove swamp so there was no escaping from the humidity. It was dreadful.

I was besieged by the Japs wanting haircuts, so I was kept busy and the cigarettes with which they paid me were always welcome.

On November 6th, we received a supply of fresh water, oil and vegetables on board, courtesy of a Japanese tanker. It was a wonderful surprise and helped to lift our spirits. When the re-supply was completed, we set off down river again. Nothing had been done to the ship. What a relief it was to reach the estuary and the sea again and feel the sea breezes. We anchored in the estuary and were joined by another eight ships and two destroyers. We set off at 1600 hours on November 7th. The sky was heavy and overcast and we ran straight into heavy seas. It was unnerving. The ship pitched and tossed and we were thrown around. This continued into the night and then - PANIC. The SS Tokyo Maru was hit by an extremely large wave.

Pandemonium reigned. My face was kicked by an S.T.C. lad trying to reach the ladder to get out of the hold. He was one of many and the air was full of shouting and swearing. It was pitch dark in the hold and nobody knew what was happening. I managed to get hold of my precious hand torch and shone it round. All of those trying to reach the ladder were being thrown around by the tossing and pitching of the ship. Fortunately, with the help of the torchlight, I was able to calm things down until first light at any rate.

By the morning, everyone was sick, including myself. I was shaken up and desperately needed to rest. I found a life raft on the main deck and lay down on that, hunger forgotten for a bit while I lay in the sun cursing my misfortune. I felt sorry for myself. The ship was still rolling around and I was given the job of organising stoking parties, a task made all the more onerous by the pitching of the vessel and the state of the men. Fortunately the storm moved on and the fury of the sea abated.

The next day, November 8th saw our first burial at sea. Corporal Allen had been suffering from ulcers and dysentery. He just seemed to give up the will to live. We all felt sad as we watched his body being banished to the waves.

Friday, November 13th was indeed a black day for me. I felt ill, really ill and, to make matters worse, it poured with rain all day. Despite feeling so weak, I had little choice but find myself a dry spot in which to stand. The only alternative was to lie in the water that was slopping around in the hold. I couldn't sleep that night and, to make matters worse, the sea was getting rough again. That night, a Dutchman died from dysentery. A second Dutchman died on the 15th. He had been lying there and nobody had realised that he was dead. His body was taken off the boat for burial at Formosa the next day.

There were many other cases of dysentery on board. The Japs were suffering as well as the P.O.W.s. Unfortunately, the only medicine we had was quinine and aspirin. When we arrived off Formosa, orders were issued for all the sick men to be taken ashore. By this time the rain had settled to a steady downpour. I went on deck for a short while but it took a terrific effort on my part to climb the ladder. I returned to the hold in no time and was only too pleased to get under my blanket. I felt too weak to do anything else.

The smell from the buckets in our hold was revolting by then but we had to put up with them. They were such essential items. There were no fewer than fifteen men in our hold suffering from dysentery out of 87 serious cases on board and 190 that were considered to be not quite so serious. There was no expertise on board to deal with the outbreak and no proper medication. There were two Dutch Javanese doctors on board. No matter how hard they tried, their efforts proved useless.

Two more deaths occurred on the night of November 18th, one R.A.F. and one army. It didn't help when we discovered the Japs were using Red Cross tinned milk that had been meant for us. They tore the labels off first but we knew what they were doing and we felt bitter about it. That milk could have helped save lives.

That night, every man was issued with an orange. The fruit had been bought by the officers with money that they kept in a fund. I added some of the juice to the rice water and it made it a little more palatable. That day there were two more deaths, one Dutch, the other R.A.F. - a man called Craig.

The Japs then had the cheek to try and sell us Form X (toilet paper) from our own supplies. To their credit though, they did bring oranges and melons on board for distribution.

Rain drenched us again and continued right through the night into the 20th. I spent the night sitting on my kit bag. We hadn't seen any sunshine since we had docked at Formosa, just continuous rain. That day two more men died, another Dutchman and a R.A.F. aircraftsman, ACI W.C. Livett. They were buried prior to our leaving Formosa at 1800 hours but before we left, another aircraftsman, D.H. Fryer passed away. Death was becoming too frequent a visitor.

The number of cases of sickness continued to increase. That night, a sick Dutchman, sitting on a bucket in the upper hold, fell over backwards into the lower hold. None of us dared touch him in case we made his injuries worse. He died during the early hours of the next morning.

Nobody seemed to care about anything or anyone any more.

Buckets for the use of diarrhoea and dysentery were lined round the hatch opening. There really was nowhere else to put them. Unfortunately the buckets would sometimes be knocked over and the contents would be spilled over the bodies lying below. We were in such a state that we just accepted this as inevitable and inescapable. There was nothing we could do about it. That reflected the state of our minds.

We had an issue of cigarettes, a packet of ten to share between four men at a cost of fifteen cents, as we found ourselves being tossed about in rough seas yet again. Fortunately we were heading into the swell this time rather than across it but it caused a lot of the men to suffer from sea sickness which, together with all their other ailments, was making them really ill. It was difficult to find enough volunteers to act as orderlies. 300 personnel were suffering from varying degrees of dysentery and diarrhoea and there had been twelve deaths since we had embarked. It was rumoured that we would be docking at an island south off Japan to off-load the Dutch. They did seem to be marginally worse affected.

The weather had become noticeably cooler. The sea was calmer and, at long last, my cold lessened considerably. Sadly, an Australian Air Force man died. He choked to death and three more men died from dysentery. I wondered if it would ever stop. To escape the smell and anger from falling buckets, I slept on deck that night, sheltering beneath a lorry. I might have escaped the smell but it didn't help me escape the cold and it was cold.

November 23rd and we were told that we could be making port the following day to off-load the Dutch contingent. Squadron Leader Grant traded his gold cufflinks to get some pineapple and milk for the sick some of which he gave to me to distribute as I thought fit. 60 men in our hold were still sick out of the 180 total. We had 18 S.T.C. lads and I kept them busy in an effort to help them forget their seasickness. We were shocked to wake the following morning and hear that Fl. Lt. Groves had died during the night. He had been one of the fittest men on board. We had noticed that his throat was swollen but he hadn't complained so we had thought no more about it. Another familiar person was lost to us.

The M.O. decided to hold a general health inspection that morning. During the inspection we passed an island and saw our first bird since leaving Formosa. Then we were joined by a lone destroyer. Thirty one days after embarking on the S.S. Tokyo Maru, we anchored at Nagasaki at 1600 hours. The high winds had dropped and it wasn't quite as cold but we couldn't get warm all day. There was to be another health inspection the next day followed by a two day wait and then a twelve hour trip. It was not stated where this trip was to take us.

On November 26th, we sailed further north for a couple of days before stopping at 1230 hours when Nip doctors boarded to carry out sanitary tests on a few cases of the seriously ill. While they were on board, Sergeant Missen died and someone stole the sick bay's supply of sugar together with a tin of milk. It was so cold. I couldn't get warm. I ducked under my blanket for the afternoon until I was wanted to shave two of the Japs. They paid me with five cigarettes and two pieces of dried fish. The fish was delicious although it was cold by the time I ate it. I ate one piece and gave the other away.

The cold was dreadful. It seemed to penetrate every part of my body and to make matters worse, I suffered from stomach ache and I couldn't shake off my cold. The ship was travelling along the coast and I couldn't help comparing it with the Cornish coast back home.

By Friday, November 27th, there had been 25 deaths on board. Sanitary tests were carried out on everyone on board. We had to stand stark naked on the upper deck while a cutting wind blew. the most embarrassing thing about the ordeal was that the medics were women. No sooner were the tests over than we packed our kitbags ready to disembark. We had arrived at a Japanese dock. As quietly as we had been given the order to leave Semplak, so also were we quietly ordered to disembark. At last we were able to leave the hell hole of a ship that we had inhabited for 33 days.

(1)

(1) Details as on pages 119 to 120

Chapter Five
The Japanese Mainland
and Mitsushima Camp

We waited on the dock side at Hanaoka close to the railway sidings while the Customs officials checked the contents of our kitbags. They stamped all cigarette packets and cigars, if anyone was lucky enough to still have any. They even stamped playing cards much to our amusement until hailstones brought us back to reality again. Those hailstones had the effect of making the conditions colder and more miserable even though we felt happy to be off that dreadful ship and back on terra firma again.

When the Customs officials had completed their checks, we repacked our bags and started a long walk to a ferry boat on which we embarked at 1830 hours on Friday, November 27th 1942. The ferry boat was almost luxurious compared to the S.S. Tokyo Maru from which we had embarked only a few hours before. It was only a very short taste of luxury as it ferried us across to Shimonoseki on the Japanese mainland of Honshu. Lunch boxes containing rice barley, seaweed and daikon, a kind of large radish, were collected en route. Some small shrimplike fish were also included and, although they were cold, they were very acceptable. Life seemed to be looking up again.

When we left the ferry, we boarded a train for the next part of our journey and we immediately started to thaw out. The train was heated. After days of bitter cold aboard the Tokyo Maru, the carriage seemed to be heated to the point of stuffiness and it became even stuffier as the night wore on. Outside the cold grew more intense.

We ate the food we were given along with cold water to drink and were surprised to realise how much we enjoyed it. Food that we could enjoy twice in one day was more than we had expected. We had had more slop and inedible rations than we cared to remember.

Our Nip interpreter, (a red cap - military policeman), spoke very good American English. He'd picked it up while studying in America before the war. This was really helpful to us on the journey. Sadly our sick were finding the journey more than they could tolerate.

We travelled through the night. Unfortunately, we had to change trains which meant we had to wait outside the station at a place called Himeji in full view of the public. We had arrived at 0545 when it was still dark and it was bitterly cold. Cold water and cold food was brought to us and, thankfully, hot tea. Even the effect of that warmth didn't last long and most of us resorted to walking up and down to encourage warmth back into our bodies. Our clothing was completely inadequate for the Japanese climate at that time of the year. I was better off then most. I had taken a suit of R.A.F. blues with me but they didn't keep me sufficiently free from the effects of the bitterly cold weather. I had nothing warm to wear under the suit. Most of the lads only had khaki drill, shorts or long trousers. Some of them had only ever served in the tropics and had never been issued with or had need of warm clothing. I felt sorry for them. I was really suffering from the cold. I dread to think how they felt.

We entrained at 0900 hours but this time the train wasn't heated. As we travelled through the countryside, we seemed to be going through endless paddy fields and limestone quarries with the occasional factory. There wasn't a sign of cattle anywhere.

We passed through the shipbuilding city of Kobe and noticed how warmly dressed the people were, particularly the soldiers. The stations along the line seemed to be modern and well constructed. Factories too seemed to be well built. We couldn't help noticing the Japanese women and commenting on how picturesque they looked in their colourful, national costume. We noticed that lorries were using gas instead of petrol. Electrically powered trains and trams were in evidence. The rail carriages seemed to be similarly constructed to our own. We went past the stations of Osaka, Kyoto and Maibara where we caught our first sight of snow capped mountains.

Sunshine broke through in mid morning and the sight of it warmed the atmosphere in the carriage. I managed to clean my teeth, shave and wash while we were on the train. We were lucky to have water on board even though it was very cold. It wasn't suitable to drink though. I felt refreshed after washing.

We were hoping that we would be issued with warmer clothing when we reached our destination and better food. Memories of our voyage from Singapore made us shudder. Without doubt, it had been the lowest level of existence any of us had ever experienced. The memories of the revolting

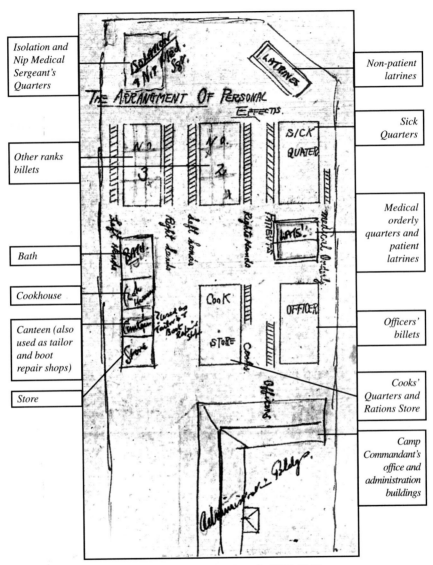

Isolation and Nip Medical Sergeant's Quarters

Other ranks billets

Bath

Cookhouse

Canteen (also used as tailor and boot repair shops)

Store

Non-patient latrines

Sick Quarters

Medical orderly quarters and patient latrines

Officers' billets

Cooks' Quarters and Rations Store

Camp Commandant's office and administration buildings

Mitsushima Camp, Tokyo Detached Nº 3, 1943
A sketch I made of the layout of our new camp which I retained
with my diaries just in case it was needed later

38

smells alone stayed with us for a long time.

Leading Aircraftsman (LAC). Taylor died on the train. He had been very ill at the start of the journey. The Japs seemed very concerned about his death and his body was moved in a blanket when we changed trains yet again at 1745 hours. Concern was shown for the health of the rest of the party.

There was only a short walk to our next train which was electrically operated. There were only two coaches to it and it was packed. It was a two hour journey and we seemed to arouse considerable interest judging by the faces of the Jap citizens who kept peering at us through the communication doors. At 2030 hours, we all had to disembark and clamber up a mountain side until we had passed over a tunnel through which we should have travelled. Apparently it was blocked. The climb was a nightmare. I was carrying my full pack and, in addition, took hold of Gunner Casey who was unable to stand without support. We had many sick personnel with us and had been told that the walk would only take half an hour. In fact, it was a two mile hike in pitch black darkness with only paper lanterns held by the guards to light the path. My own precious torch proved invaluable because the paths were exceptionally tricky and treacherous. However we finally climbed back down and on to another train that was waiting at the other end. Three quarters of an hour later, we arrived at our final destination, Hiraoka station.

Again we found we had to face another walk to the camp. "Only a few minutes,' we were told. We soon proved them wrong. But at last, we arrived at our new camp, Mitsushima Camp. We were exhausted. All we wanted to do was lie down and sleep but that luxury was not to be ours. First of all we had to sign another oath of obedience after being treated to a very noisy speech by our new Camp Commandant. He warned us that we must remember we were at war and couldn't expect too much. He also warned us about trying to escape. We were almost asleep on our feet but it did come to an end and we were issued with five camp blankets, one English army tunic or battledress, a pair of battledress trousers, overall type, and a grey flannel shirt. The temperature was already bordering on freezing. Exhaled breath turned into clouds of steam. The pressed blankets were cold and damp to the touch. But at last, at 0100 hours on November 29th, we were allowed to retire to our bed spaces with the knowledge that we would have to be up at 0530 hours for the first Tenko of the day. I shared a bed space with Les Fullick. We were exhausted and hungry. I opened a tin of Heinz stew which had been given to me by an STC lad on the boat, bless him. He was never to know how much it meant. Les and I soon made short work of the tin's contents and, in no time at all, slept. There was no lurching of the bed space, no falling slop buckets, no drenching rain. It was bliss.

We started work on November 30th. We had been excused work on our first day at Mitsushima Camp. Instead we had been roused at 0515 for our first Tenko and we had had to fill in yet more forms, about footwear this time, not my favourite occupation at that time in the morning. Then came the first shock. We had to undergo a medical check. The members of our hut had to assemble outside, stark naked. It was bitterly cold and a keen wind was blowing. We were weighed and our feet, chest and height measurements were taken and we were expected to say thank you to our Nip captors for that!

Our first meal at the camp was a vegetable stew and rice mixed with barley. I don't know whether it was something in the stew or what but I had a wicked attack of diarrhoea following that. To make matters worse, I also caught a chill in the stomach. What a life! I thought with longing of home.

The next day, we were roused at 0600 hours, breakfast was at 0630 and work parade at 0700 hours. I was wearing hand made sandals on my feet and my big toe was really sore so I was assigned work in the camp. Scurvy had broken out and the first case of diphtheria had been notified.

White frost covered the area and there was little chance of the sun breaking through the clouds that day. Mitsushima Camp was situated in a valley surrounded by mountains. Americans had been interned there before us and they had suffered very heavy losses among their personnel, mainly from disease.

The next day we were allowed to light a fire outside one of the untenanted huts and we were given an issue of bread. It was given to each of us in a large lump and it was delicious. I'd almost forgotten the taste of it. I was drooling at the lips when I smelt it. I toasted some over the fire and it was lusho. The Nips told us that we would be given bread three days in every ten. That was really something to look forward to.

When the sun did break through, it was very hot. That was generally between 1030 and 1530 hours each day but, as soon as it disappeared behind the mountains, the vicious cold returned with a vengeance.

Later on, the Nips handed out glucose solution for injecting those of us with chronic diarrhoea. Maybe some of them were humane after all.

I had a quiet time on that first work day, so I took the opportunity to wash and dry my socks and get under my blankets for a rest. This was forbidden officially and, just as I was settling down, a Japanese guard walked in. It was just my luck. I staggered to my feet and he went out. I was lucky!

We weren't to have tea, just hot water to drink and in which to wash the dishes. That was great. Then we were told that the water at the wash stand was contaminated with cholera and dysentry germs, wonderful!

My tongue and throat became swollen and sore because there wasn't enough to drink. I gargled and drank as much as I could but it wasn't enough. The stew helped. Some of the others couldn't even swallow that because their throats were so swollen so there was plenty for those who could. We worked in a quarry, breaking and loading rock and stone. Working in a quarry each day didn't help.

It was hard, physically taxing, dusty work. An avalanche on my first day at the quarry didn't give us any excuse to slow down. We hadn't done any physical work for a long time and working with tools of which we had little or no experience was no joke. We worked from 0700 hours until midday, then from 1300 hours until 1700 hours. By the end of the working day, we were exhausted.

I reported to the Japanese sergeant that the stew was much too thin. He promised to look into the complaint and, at the same time, he asked me for a sketch of myself. They really were a strange race. Then he told me I looked like Cary Grant, a famous American film star. Later on, he told me that I was the most handsome man on the camp. I began to get worried! Still he did give me a cigarette and shook my hand.

Pilot Officer Bruce died from diphtheria that first week and, much to our surprise, the Japs paid their respects. His remains were cremated the next day while we were at work in the quarry.

The work we were doing seemed to be aimed at changing the course of a river and I began to wonder if the end product would be to construct a dam. The tools, scrapers and rakes we used were of poor quality, mostly made of wood - bamboo. Stones were put into bamboo baskets which were tipped into trucks when they were full. Fortunately electric motors were used to haul the trucks carrying the stone from the quarry.

At a temperature of 30 degrees Fahrenheit or below, it was very cold and, to make life more miserable, my mouth was very sore and ulcerated.

The diarrhoea had stopped. Instead I was suffering from flatulence. The stew we were given didn't help and it was a relief when I managed to eat a piece of toast but my mouth was so sore it took a lot of effort to swallow it.

The Nip Warrant officer appointed 'hanchos' to be in charge of each hut. I was the hancho for hut 2. I was required to wear two linen labels which showed 'Works no. 25/2 - 51/2 which was my group and hut number.

Pneumonia and dysentry took the life of Corporal Cross on December 3rd. Again, he was cremated whilst we were at work in the quarry. It was bitterly cold that day and work stopped at 1615 hours because of the heavy rain. Also on that day, without explanation, pay sheets were distributed.

I was still wearing my hand made sandals. Trying to wear the footwear that the Japs supplied was useless. They were far too small for European feet. My sandals weren't suitable for the work in the quarry and my toe was really sore and the bickering between the STC lads and our chaps only added to the problems. Trying to sort them all out with a sore throat, tongue and mouth didn't help. I did manage to get an extra ration of bread for the sick men. For some unknown reason, the Japs seemed to think that sick men did not need to be fed. They only needed rice water.

Corporal Skelton died the following day from pneumonia. Three deaths in three days was unnerving. I had caught another heavy cold to accompany my sore throat and mouth and working in the freezing quarry didn't help. When we returned to the hut, we were allowed to light a fire in the middle of the floor but there was no hole for the smoke to escape which left us coughing our hearts out. I had to go to the latrines twice during that night and it was a freezing experience. I had no proper shoes to wear, neither the time nor materials to make any.

Gunner Mackie died on December 6th. There were too many deaths and too many ailments and I was no exception. The diet was playing havoc with my stomach. Tiffin that day was cold cabbage and fish and the usual rice and barley. No water was available to us in the morning and icicles were hanging from every conceivable point. The day was exceptionally cold and my throat and mouth were so bad, I could hardly speak or swallow and I realised most of the other men were in the same state. There were no medical supplies but we had seen a Red Cross delivery being made to the camp. We were made to run round the huts the next morning to get warm and to work harder at the quarry for the same reason. That certainly did not impress the Yanks that were in our working party. We were made to run to the quarry and back again. That was particularly hard for men like myself with bad feet. I suppose it did make us feel a bit warmer, not that we noticed at the time. We were keen to dodge the butts of the rifles that the guards used to hit the laggards. In fact the Nips eased their boredom by slapping or punching us more and more for the slightest offence, even some that we didn't know we had committed. We were forced to work harder and longer at the quarry as well. We were allowed drinks of hot water, the only liquid available during the working day but the over-all dryness soon returned. It was more akin to a Chinese torture. How we longed for a cup of good old English tea.

A Japanese medical officer was visiting the camp at this time but he wasn't much help to us. He sent the sick to work except for the really ill and he dosed those that were suffering from diarrhoea with Epsom salts. The orders that the Commandant of the Camp issued did little to improve morale. They read ;

Attention to the Prisoners.

1. You may not let slip your memory that you are prisoners even for a moment.

2. If you should do an act of a complaint or discontent I will punish you as follows, note:

a. anyone who complains as regards the meal will be reduced one's diet or be fasted.

b. Whoever complains to the garment or other granted goods will be punished with a grave guard room.

c. Anyone who does a breach of military discipline or who is following another blindly and a strife will be punished with a felony or a shooting.

D. Without any reason, anyone who loathes to serve in a labour, will be punished with a felony.

Warning

You should be resolved that even if you may be an officer, I forbid eating the bread of idleness and order serving to a labour or other diligent service.

Orders of Nipponese Commander,
Mitsushima Camp.

(see over)

The weather became even colder on December 9th and the ground was frozen solid. I don't think anyone who hasn't experienced it can under-

Attention in the Prisoner   8/12/42.

1. You must not let slip from memory that you (eve) are prisoners even for a moment.

2. If you should do an act of a complaint or discontent. I will punish you as follows. note:-

(I) Anyone who complains as regards the meal will be reduced one's diet or be fasted.

II. Whoever complains to the garment or other granted goods, will be punished with a grave guard-room.

III. Anyone who does a breach of Military discipline or who is following another blindly and a strife, will be punished with a felony or a shooting.

IV. Without any reason, anyone who loathes to serve in a labour, will be punished with a felony.

Warning:-

You should be resolved that even if you may be a officer, I forbid eating the bread of idleness and order serving to a labour or other diligent service.

ORDERS of
N. Japanese Commander
MATSHIMA CAMP.

No 3. P.O.W. Camp.
TOKYO DETACHED.

We deliberately left the 'Japanese English' when copying orders

44

stand how dreadful the cold was and how it affected us. It penetrated the whole of our bodies right into our bones until they ached with the pain. It became an effort to move, to put one foot in front of the other and, for people like myself without proper shoes, it was sheer agony. My toe was really painful but I had little choice except to suffer with it.

By the following evening it was so painful that I defied camp rules and crawled between my blankets before 0630. I couldn't put up with the pain any longer, a pain that increased the longer I stood around. Lying down was the nearest I could get to some relief.

There was one bright light. The rumour had spread that we would only be at the camp for another two months. Then we'd be moved to a larger camp and, hopefully, better conditions. We just prayed that we'd still be around at the end of those two months.

I managed to see the Nip doctor on the morning of December 11th. The next day I wasn't required to work. At last I had a chance to rest and I needed it. There was no time off. Working seven days a week was the order of the day. Even though I was excused work, I still had to go to the quarry. I had been given aspirins that I was to take three times a day. My tongue was still very painful and my throat was so sore that I had great difficulty in swallowing. To make matters worse, my glands were swollen. Because the pipes were frozen there was no water and I was desperate for something to drink. Trying to swallow the aspirins without water was an ordeal. To take my mind off my aches and pains, I tried to eat as much as I could find. Eating was OK but swallowing was a different matter altogether. We were given too little rice in our food and too much barley and that didn't help but there were plenty of onions both boiled and raw.

I was given another days rest on December 13th. The Dutch doctor had no medicine to help us. His task seemed to be saying if we were fit for work or not. The Japanese guards were of the bullying type. They would harry the sick men to work and keep them there until they collapsed and had to be carried back to the camp.

I returned to work on December 14th. It was not one of my happiest days. Four more men died that day, two in hospital and two in the camp adding to the death of Gunner Casey who had died the previous day. The incidence of death had become intolerable. Good men were being taken from us. None of us deserved what we had to put up with least of all the deaths of our comrades.

We started to experience a most unpleasant form of Japanese behav iour. One of the guards resorted to punching everybody's faces and he seemed to relish doing so. Hitting us with a clenched fist was the way we were punished for the slightest reason. Sometimes we didn't know what we'd done wrong. Others would hit us across the head with a sword shaped stick so hard that they could knock a person unconscious. Not all the guards behaved like this but those that did seemed to *enjoy* acting like that.

One day, we were lined up in two lines opposite each other and then we were told to hit each other which we did half heartedly. That didn't satisfy the guards. They made us punch harder and harder until we were really hurting each other and that was because a man had broken a plate. More serious offences such as stealing or fighting were dealt with by the officers. Some of the Americans seemed to go out of their way to irritate the Japs.

Christmas was drawing nearer and I couldn't help thinking with longing of the Christmases we had had at home and wondering what my family was doing. It didn't help that our rations had been cut right back. Without exception, everyone was cold, hungry, weak and understandably miserable. For breakfast we had been given a slice of bread and 'soup'. I couldn't stop myself moaning to the foreman on the job about the poor meals. I didn't expect it to go any further but it paid off a little. That evening we did have a slight increase in quantity. But the grub was short again the next day! I felt annoyed that I had to speak up for the men like that. Our officers should have been doing it. They didn't have to work like we lesser mortals did.

Corporal Singleton died on December 18th. We had become far too accustomed to death and, sadly, his passing hardly raised an eyebrow. Survival was more important to us by then. I was the Under Officer of the Day (U.O.D.) and managed to get that extra rice from the cooks. It was burnt but that did not worry anyone, every grain was hungrily devoured.

I followed this up with some hair cutting much to the approval of the Nip Warrant Officer. A Japanese Colonel was visiting the camp at the time and he seemed pleased with what he saw. He obviously felt moved sufficiently to declare that we would not have to work on Christmas Day and that there would be an orange each, extra bread and tobacco and the use of a hot bath. There was a spontaneous round of cheers but he had to spoil it by saying that idle men would not get those things.

I cut some of the officers' hair that day and the hair 'and the lice' of some of the Yanks this and earned the princely sum of five cigarettes. I also got paid for performing the duties of UOD that day. Any addition to my meagre savings was welcome.

There was insufficient food and the cold was made even colder by the wind blowing through every nook and cranny in the hut. The pain in my toe was getting worse again. Mind you, it was so cold underfoot, I wonder there was any feeling left in my toe. We heard that American Walsh had died but my mind had grown numb and I was having difficulty remembering how many men we had lost. It was all too depressing. My mind was soon distracted from the exercise when one of the cooks brought in some extra rice, barley and stew from the mess. A mad rush ensued to get a share of the extra food. The lads were so desperate for a feed they ate anything. What a pitiful sight the rush for food made.

There was absolutely no let up at work on Christmas Eve. Because we had been promised the day off for Christmas, the Nips made us work all the harder the day before. I suppose, however, that it helped us to make that first Christmas Day in captivity all the more valuable to us.

The first Tenko of the day took place an hour later than usual. That gave us a calmer start to the day. We were treated to a little extra soup at breakfast. It didn't taste any different but it did help to calm our hunger

Christmas 'Celebrations' at Mitsushima Camp 1942. No, the lads were not all trying to grab a share of the grub on the table. There just was not enough to go around. The lads are gathered around to have the photograph taken and it says a lot for the lads that they could still work up a smile despite the conditions they were having to endure. I am at the centre back (arrowed) and obviously too far back for the camera's depth of focus.

Christmas 1942 at Mitsushima Camp, Tokyo Nº 3 Area, when some Japs insisted on being photographed with senior prisoners. From the left is a mean natured Camp Guard, an English officer, a Canadian Officer, the Camp Commandant, an American Officer, a second English Officer and the Japanese Medical Officer - the only decent Jap there.

Making the most of a sad situation the lads put on a Christmas pantomime at Mitsushima Camp, for Christmas 1942. The music stands were manufactured by yours truly - William C Rose RAFVR.

pangs from which we were all suffering. This was followed by a commendation parade and a speech by the Japanese Commanding Officer.

Presentations were made to those who had work chits, mainly to those who had not been off sick. I only had two which earned me ten cigarettes.

We received half a loaf of bread each at Tiffin and one very hot, curried stew. I decided the menu had been designed to burn off any throat infection we might have had.

We weren't given any time for a Christmas Service as we had requested and the Nips made us crop our hair before we were allowed into the communal bath. If we objected, they took great delight in tearing our hair off themselves. I cropped several of the lads hair for them but it was all done in a hurry and I didn't have time to take the usual care over the task. I got one of the others to crop my hair for me. Mind you, it was necessary for a lot of men. Some of them were in a very dirty condition. They couldn't be otherwise when you thought of the unhygienic state in which we were living. They had developed lice and various other skin complaints.

The hot bath was heaven but considering the length of time we had endured without being able to have a complete wash, it was all too short.

Unfortunately, the body heat it had encouraged didn't last long once I got out but it was bliss while it lasted.

Then we were issued with four copies of the Nippon Times. We soon discovered the reason for this largesse. Each paper placed considerable emphasis on the losses experienced by the Allies as a result of Japanese attacks (ie. Sinking of HMS Prince of Wales and HMS Repulse) - resulting in utter despondency at such losses. How could we expect release and return home? We were eating our evening meal, when we were suddenly ordered outside and told to gather round a bonfire and we were ordered to sing to entertain our Japanese captors. As if that wasn't enough, they made the young Indians from the STC group perform a dance round the fire like Red Indians did in the movies. They were reluctant and embarrassed and so were we. Like all of us, they had lost a lot of weight and were almost skeletal in appearance. To see them trying to perform in this way was one of the most pathetic sights I have ever seen in my life.

I don't think any of us went to sleep that night without thinking of previous Christmases we had spent and wondering about our families back at home.

It was back to work on Boxing Day. The day's rest had done us good but it didn't do anything to ease the cold or the hunger. Then I hit my bad toe with a sledgehammer. Boy, oh boy, did it hurt but it took my mind off other things, for a while at least. That evening we were each issued with two small oranges and some small cakes. Anything extra in the food line was always welcome, and oranges, however small, were particularly so.

The next day, we were allowed to hand in postcards we had written to send home. They weren't the two page letters we had been promised we could send but they were something. I gave mine in with a silent prayer that it would reach Joyce then, to our surprise, we were given a second issue of two oranges. Somebody must have told them it was the custom to have oranges at Christmas time. This was followed by a kit inspection. The only good thing about that was that it was conducted in our huts rather than standing out in the bitter cold and the following day, December 28th, was incredibly cold. We had to carry stones in a basket slung on a pole between two of us. The task wasn't made any easier by my inadequate footwear. The pain in my toes was excruciating.

During the day, a Yank earned himself a beating. We were told that he had been caught stealing. I hadn't any idea what he had stolen, nor had anyone else for that matter. Life was getting beyond any sort of tolerance level. The next day was colder still and I was surprised that there were no accidents. There might well have been if a fire had not been lit during tiffin but we were ordered back to work after ten minutes. We hadn't had time to thaw out.

We knew that Red Cross parcels had arrived at the camp but we hadn't seen any sign of them. I did wonder about those small oranges though. They had been issued soon after one of the men had seen the parcels arrive. On New Year's Eve the Nips decorated the Camp buildings with foliage and paper chains ready for the New Year's Day celebrations. They told us that we would have three days rest. We would believe that when it happened. But I remember that evening for a completely different event. A mess orderly accidentally broke a window in the cookhouse. That earned him and everybody else in the hut a punch on the jaw from the Japanese cooks. I became the target of a blow from a larger than normal cook and it hurt. A couple of days later one of the Japs broke a dish in the kitchen. For that, he was punched on the chin by a corporal. Then the sergeant punched the corporal and a more senior officer punched the sergeant and so on, finishing when they all shook hands. What a strange people they were. Later on, we were each issued with a pair of green overalls. They looked more like art silk pyjamas than working overalls, nevertheless, they were very welcome. I was out at work when other clothing was issued and Les Fulluck spoke up for me and secured a RAF blue overcoat and a pair of socks that had belonged to LAC Almeroth,

A sleet storm that afternoon made working conditions extremely miserable as we unloaded sand and cement from trucks. I got yet another cold, probably from getting cold after the hot bath and, because I still had no boots. My toe would not heal properly and that added to the misery.

The Nip interpreter had earned himself the nickname of 'Mushymouth' and he had turned into a real fiend each day around Tenko time. He relieved his frustrations by taking it out on all of us and December 31st was no exception. Over the previous three days, our meals had been late and we had had to eat them in a hurry. That day was no exception but the cook did dish out a little laggi (extra). The evening meal was raw onion and rice, a diet that was playing absolute havoc with our bowels. I had been given a small orange by the foreman at work which made a very welcome addition. As I fell asleep that night, I thanked the Lord that 1942 was finally coming to an end. There we were, thousands of miles away from our homes and families, freezing cold, starving, humiliated and most of us in poor health with not one bit of news from home or on how the world was getting on without us. We felt forgotten. It had certainly been the worst year of my life.

1943 dawned and we found the Japanese honouring their word and giving us a three-day break. No work was scheduled to take place for those three days. It was a wonderful start to 1943. To make the start of the New Year even better, Red Cross parcels were issued with a packet of five cigarettes for each man, I don't think anyone can understand what those parcels meant to us. They brought happiness and hope. Time and time again, I heard the words, "Thank God for the Red Cross". Strangely enough the parcels had been packed in Bermondsey, London, the place where I had been born. Seeing the name printed on the box brought tears to my eyes and memories of my old home town came crowding into my mind.

We started the day with a mid morning hot bath and then addressed ourselves to our Red Cross parcels. Each parcel comprised a box 14 x 7 x 5 inches. Mine contained a tin of biscuits, a marmalade pudding, a tin of Nestles milk, a quarter pound bar of Needler's superfine plain chocolate, a small tin of cheese, a tin of apricot jam, tinned turkey and tongue paste, two packets of Maypole tea, eight ounces of tinned bacon, a tin of tomatoes, a tin of beef stew and vegetables and a quarter pound of margarine. What a box of goodies that was.

Les Fulluck and I shared our boxes. That way we avoided any loss or

51

extravagant waste when opening tins. We were also able to enjoy a greater assortment of food, such as syrup, creamed rice and more tomatoes to go with the bacon. Most of the men shared their goodies with friends in the same way.

The lads were happier on New Year's day than they had been for a long time. The Red Cross parcels had given us some real food to eat and, for men like us who had been subject to a considerable degree of starvation, it was wonderful. Fires were permitted in the huts all day and, as a result, there was a lot of cooking and tea making. We drank real tea instead of just plain hot water. It was the taste of luxury but it reminded us of home and brought back memories of Blighty as did the smell of frying bacon and tomatoes. Nobody cared that the hut was full of smoke. It was worth putting up with the discomfort of it. There was only one thing that spoiled it for me. I went down with a heavy cold. I should never have had that bath!

The January 2nd and our second day of rest was again marked by the aroma of cooking, bacon, tomatoes and, strangely enough, rice. An egg or two would have gone down well but whoever would have wanted rice! At midday I had marmalade pudding and a fresh brew of tea. It was delicious but it reminded me of the wonderful steamed puddings my Joycie used to make. But I couldn't last the day. My cold was so bad that I had to crawl back into bed and try and sleep it off. I got up in time for Tenko the next morning but I felt strange and heady. I still managed some dhobi (washing clothes) in cold water of course and I fed myself some biscuits spread with margarine and syrup, delicious! I also managed to eat some gelatine with the usual issue of barley. It was a strange mixture but it added to the variety of food.

But, all too soon, those three days of rest were over. January 4th was another cold, miserable day and, once again, the rice issue was short. I suppose they thought we could make up the shortfall from food in our Red Cross parcels. We were back to a diet of soup which contained horse meat and leeks. Fortunately Les and I still had some of our parcels left so we were able to supplement the poor diet. So were the Japs. They drank sake. When we returned to camp, we found the cook boozed out of this world lying up in the cookhouse.

The previous evening, 24 Yanks had been put into the guardroom (ESO), for refusing to get up in time for Tenko. To be put in ESO was like being put in dog kennels or vegetable crates, 5 feet by 5 feet by 4 feet. They stayed there for twenty four hours without food or water but were released in time to start work back in the quarry. It was back to hard labour. My cold hadn't improved and, to cap everything else, I had developed piles. Misery, depression and ill health had found its way back into our lives. I weighed in at 59 kilograms, (a tad over nine stone). We were all skin and bones. Some of the men were little more than walking skeletons. The Camp Commandant made another inspection and, following this, Les and I tucked into a meal of beef and veg with gelatine. We followed that up with a tin of cheese and margarine and washed it down with another cup of freshly brewed tea. We were certainly living it up.

I was shocked to hear that Corporal Street and an American had died on the 5th and 7th of January respectively. This news really disturbed me. I had thought we had left the bad times behind us in 1942, but a week into the new year and death was on our heels once more.

The water thawed out on January 9th. You have no idea what a wonderful thing this was. For a short while, water was not rationed. The Camp Commandant told us that we would have extra rice that day. He said he knew that we were hungry and then we ended up with shorter rations than ever. However I managed to trade some gelatine for a tin of milk. That was a good swap.

I had a very sore and aching leg and stomach and, after a sleepless night, I reported sick. I was issued with carbon to settle my upset stomach. It was raining so heavily that day that we couldn't work. I felt so depressed and ill that I admitted myself to the sick quarters. They gave me magnesium sulphate for my stomach,- Epsom salts! Strangely enough, it partly solved the problem. Freezing conditions returned two days later. It was bitterly cold and food was in short supply. I was beginning to feel better but very, very weak. Fortunately, barley supplies arrived at the camp the next day. Although it played havoc with our stomachs, we missed it when it wasn't included in our diet. Our bodies had become accustomed to it.

I spent some time talking to Jimmy Hepburn that afternoon and that got me thinking about what I would do when I got home again. It was the first time I'd given it any thought. Unfortunately, most of our talk and thoughts turned too frequently to food. We prayed constantly for a quick return home and thought often of our families and hoped they were escaping the horrors of war.

Everyone was issued with overcoats and hoods except for those of us in hospital. We had to wait until we returned to work. Fortunately we had stoves in the hut but it didn't keep the penetrating cold completely out. We had barley and dried fish that night and that was a bonus.

More snow fell on January 16th. I was beginning to feel better. Then the Nip interpreter declared that diarrhoea patients would only be allowed two meals of a little wet rice each day. Les Fulluck sold a half crown piece for one and a half yen and I was able to buy a rice issue from a Yank. I had another long talk with Jimmy Hepburn that night, about pig keeping. The next day, I moved my bed to the centre aisle, away from the diarrhoea patients. That way, I was entitled to three meals a day.

While I was in the sick bay, a young STC lad called Chan was caught stealing. He was given the opportunity to own up and, when he refused, he was handed over to the Japs. They got the truth out of him and then beat him up. He was sentenced to 20 days in the guard room during which, he was to be woken every two hours.

Another pay day came round and I was due money for 25 days. I received 2yen 5sen. At Tenko we were allowed to purchase a packet of biscuits and some candy if we had diligence chits. We had to pay for it, 10 sen. I also managed to buy some cod liver oil capsules. Yet, I had this feeling that something good was going to happen. I don't know how or why I felt that but the feeling was so strong that it was almost overpowering and then, at last, we did have some good news. We were told that we were leaving there on February 1st. But it turned out to be another rumour.

I returned to work on the last day of January. I felt better and, thankfully, we were still receiving extra rations. It was bitter cold and a strong wind was blowing and when we got to work we found all the fires had been put out. We weren't even able to warm ourselves at the end of a day's work.

February 1st was a day of disappointment. There was no more talk of leaving the camp and I fell into the river. Fortunately, it was only my feet that were soaked. I managed to grab hold of a rope above the walkway. It was lucky I did. The river was fast flowing and used to float tree trunks down to the timber yards. I wouldn't have had much chance if I had finished up in that.

Out of 249 prisoners, only 144 were fit for work. For some reason Mushymouth vented his anger on me. He seemed to think it was my fault. Some Yanks were caught in their blankets after the work parade. For that, they were each subjected to a punch on the jaw. Then all the Yanks were punished by standing to attention from 1915 hours to 2000. When you consider how weak these men were, you'll realise what a harsh punish ment that was.

Another time the Americans had to stand to attention outside their hut and hold blocks of ice above their heads. They had to stand like that for two hours because one of them had offended one of the guards. To weak, underfed men, that was sheer torture. Generally the punishment was a punch or a beating. If they couldn't find the culprit, they would often select anyone and punish him as an example.

There was a very heavy fall of snow on February 3rd. but that didn't stop us having to turn out for work. Thankfully the Nips had fitted me up with a pair of boots. They were second hand but that didn't matter. They were so much better than my hand made sandals for walking through the snow. The boots that the Red Cross sent had still not been distributed. We returned from work at 2100 hours having walked through a heavy blizzard. Fortunately we were allowed to light fires although we were only allowed to use coal dust and that isn't the most warming of fuel. I dried myself at the stove at the cobbler's shop. I had had to go there to have some adjustments made to my boots. It didn't help that the rations had been further reduced for the third day. I felt very weak at work the next day. My hunger was crippling. Until one has experienced real hunger, you cannot understand how painful it is. Fortunately I was able to exchange two cigarettes for a small bowl of rice. The snow had begun to thaw and it was wet underfoot. My boots were water tight but that meant the water couldn't drain out of them and my feet stayed wet all day.

I was the winch control man when one of the guards 'Rivet Tooth' began to taunt me, "You 142 (my number) you 'abra' boy," which meant, or so I thought, that I was not working hard enough.

He followed this up by putting down his rifle and confronting me. I had had enough and I went for him. I had him on his back in no time. The rest of the detail had gathered round us and were shouting their support. Then I paused and the realisation of what I had done came into my mind. I knew I would be in for trouble, big trouble! We both scrambled to our feet and, to my surprise 'Rivet Tooth' shook my hand and said, "Rozzo, you very strong," and that was that. We went back to work as if nothing had happened. It would have been a different matter if one of the senior guards had seen us.

Les Fulluck and myself tried a new job the following day and had to load forty trucks of ballast. Fortunately the sun came out for a while which raised our spirits and we actually had a decent cup of tea at the break. But I suffered the next day for the exertion we had used. I felt so tired and

Meirei

Order:- 10/2/43.

1) All prisoners will wear issue sheet around the stomach in 3 folds.

2) Two Officers commencing 11/2/43 will act as observers of working parties + they will take note of idle, diligent or dangerous workers. Officers on other duties such as bath masters, sacks, Officer of the day etc must not be chosen. Nipponese Guards will show place to Officers from where they will observe (this will continue until further notice) [Orders finish]

Report:- From 10/3/43 O. of Day + U.O.D read further Masters + leaders will report at 5. P.M at Admin Office. If you have nothing to report Officer of day to be advised before time noted above.

2) The Nip. Commander considers it will be better for each man to have a hot bottle on his stomach at night. Water heated in Boilers for this purpose.

3) Overalls must be worn at all times. It has been frequently found that prisoners are not wearing Clothes which are issued for above purpose?

4) All Prisoners must wear new number on Overalls. If any man found without number we report to Admin Office?

Notes:- Boiler for hot water supply was situated in open & was known to be actually boiling on about 1 Dz. occasions only. Cold water being constantly added prevented a continual supply of boiled water, yet we were ordered to drink only boiled water.

Kiho

A copy of the instruction of daily orders, telling us - 1. All prisoners will wear issue sheet around the stomach in 3 folds and 2. Two Officers commencing 11/2/43 will act as observers of working parties and they will take note of idle, dilligent or dangerous workers ...etc.

weak. The foreman tried to encourage me by giving me three cigarettes. Some food would have been better. Rations were really low and the lads were becoming short tempered and argumentative. It poured with rain so heavily that we were unable to work the following morning but it didn't give us much rest. The huts were flooded and we had to spend the day baling out. The cold conditions soon returned and the ground was so frozen that we found it impossible to dig up the gravel.

Pneumonia became evident amongst the men. Fortunately our rice ration was improved and I managed to get some extra by exchanging some cigarettes with the Yanks for part of their quota. They preferred smoking to eating. Mind you, I didn't have much time to eat it. I had been made U.O.D. yet again. The duties that were imposed on one, didn't give me much time for anything and Mushymouth chose that time to call me in and issue toothbrushes and powder, ink, paper, etc. I also found myself issued with a Japanese overcoat with a hood. That was welcome. By this time there were only 24 men left from our flight of 40 and only 80 left in the billet out of a strength of 120.

I noticed that the guards were being changed more frequently and ci

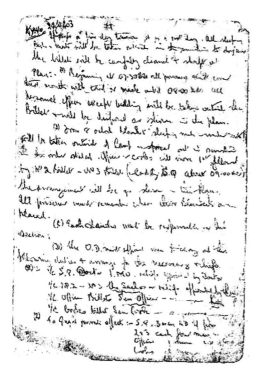

An example of the notes I took from the Kyho, or daily routine orders for the camp. These notes, were transcribed on the 24th April 1943.

vilians were often overseeing us at work. Even our own officers were given turns at supervising us. We started returning from work so that Tenko could take place earlier because the guards had to go out of camp.

We had a rest day on Sunday and a welcome bath. Then we deloused our shirts. We had been expecting fleas to appear and they did. I had one flannel shirt and one pair of pants so it was important to keep them clean. Trimming beards and cutting hair was another chore that we completed that day.

February ran into March. There wouldn't have been much to write home about in the way of cheerful news if we had been given the chance to write to our loved ones and tell them what life was really like

March started with a bit of a bang. We spent the day shifting the cables on which the buckets of gravel travelled. It was hard work and my stomach was working overtime yet again. The S.T.C. lads in my section were getting more and more difficult to handle and I was in danger of losing my temper with them. I'd just about had enough of their nonsense. And to cap it all, my mate Les was hospitalised with gastric influenza and I was given another spell on U.O.D. duties.

It was freezing cold on the Wednesday morning and we had to clean the camp ready for an inspection. In addition we were given a bath and a medical examination. My weight had dropped to eight stone ten pounds which wasn't surprising on the rations we'd been having. Nevertheless, at five foot ten inches tall, I was not a pretty sight. In the afternoon, I was occupied doing some carpentry work for the Nips, one of whom wanted the watch I was wearing on my wrist. He paid me two oranges and six packets of cigarettes for it which wasn't a bad exchange considering the watch didn't have a winder and wasn't much use.

The weather was still very cold although, when the sun rose above the mountains, it was warm enough for us to take off our jackets. We began to understand why some Japanese revered and worshipped the sun and showed respect to a Shinto God. But, although the temperature had improved, during the day at any rate, the rain certainly hadn't and there were days when we had to return to camp early because the rain was too heavy for us to carry on working. My hands had become so chapped and sore in these conditions that I resorted to rubbing them with dubbin that was meant for our boots in an effort to ease the pain.

That was another problem, boots. Mine were in such a state by this time that the soles flapped as I walked and were in danger of losing contact with the uppers altogether. One of the guards managed to find another boot but it didn't do anything to ease the problem. There was only the one boot, (I don't know what had happened to its partner), and it was far too small.

The evening meals of rice, barley with dry bean and soya bean paste were indigestible and didn't do much for my stomach, but it was food and there was never enough of it. We were always hungry. Hunger had become a part of our lives but, in particular, we were hungry for British food. I dreamed of eating a roast meal one night, roast beef, Yorkshire pudding and all that went with it and I couldn't get that thought out of my head. All the time I was working, the picture of that meal was in my head but we sat down that night to the usual, rice, barley, dried beans and soya bean paste. We could probably have coped if there had been more of it but, however we felt, we knew that our rations were larger than the Japanese villagers were receiving. We received the rations that were considered suitable for manual workers. A Jap sergeant told us that their own civilians were short of food.

Our foreman was a spiteful individual that we called Raspberry Nose. We were digging stones and rocks out of the river bank and loading them into buckets which were carried to the top of the hill by cable. It was a bitterly cold day and we gathered around a small fire during our fifteen minute break when Raspberry Nose appeared and viciously kicked it out and started beating us. The he returned to his observation post leaving us cold and dejected. He would threaten and find fault with all sorts of things.

To be fair, I don't think he was well and he did eventually take sick leave. He was replaced by a jolly little fellow who was much more relaxed and this made the guards more relaxed as well. That was when we discovered that most of them could speak some English and understood a lot of what we were saying. One of the guards became quite informative about the progress of the war.

An American officer issued us with pencils and paper to write home. We had to be careful what we said because we knew our letters would be censored. I was surprised to see some of the men staring at their paper as if they didn't know what to write, then I realised that they didn't know how to write home. They needed help to write a letter home. That happened in those days. There were plenty of people who couldn't read or write.

April started with more trouble from the STC lads as well as some other fellows, mainly American, particularly one called Jones. He was a moaner and a complainer. He was a thorn in my side and I was never able to find out what his problem was. This time, they were complaining about the way I had arranged for the rice to be distributed. The STC lads would lean over the dishes to check out that there was the same amount in each bowl. Fortunately the cook's helper sorted out the problem this time by drawing two lots of rations and trading one.

Later that day, Mushymouth officiously told us that N.C.O.s would be receiving 15 sen a day instead of ten. Any increase was welcome and although this was a pittance it did allow us to trade and buy a few extras.

The Nip behaviour was quite puzzling at times. They could be quite decent to the lads, then suddenly change and become officious or spiteful for some unknown reason. One brought me some candies and biscuits one day and insisted I ate them outside the hut and wipe every trace from my mouth so that nobody would know. Some of the guards would give us a small gift, a cigarette or an extra helping of burnt rice. Others were just as likely to swipe out at us.

It was about this time that we started receiving extra (leggi) rice with beans and vegetables from the officers' mess. So, for several successive nights, we went to bed with full stomachs. Either the officers were being fed better than we were or they were off their food.

On the fifth of the month some Red Cross supplies turned up, bully beef, dried fruit and milk powder, not that it made any difference to the diet we were given. The following day, Gunner Charman died and on the

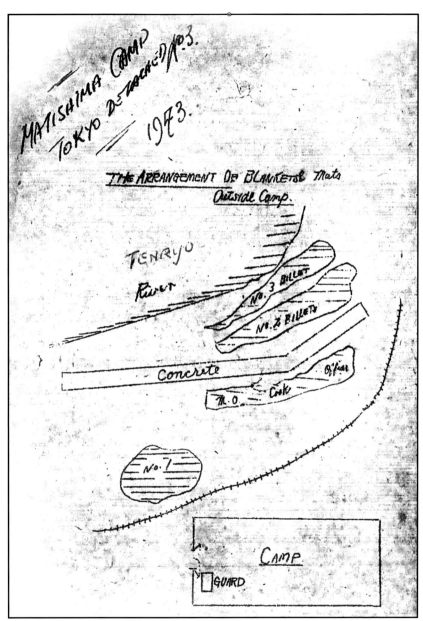

This map gives the reader some idea of the layout of the contaminated blankets for cleaning and drying

The Dam construction at Mitsushima

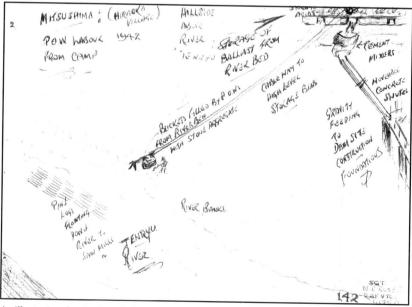

An illustration showing how the buckets of stone aggregate were transferred to the top of the dam

eighth, three of the STC lads. Although they had done nothing but cause me trouble, I was saddened by their deaths. Then we had the news that W.O. Coker had died. What with that and the fact that my pal, Les was still ill, I was in no mood to deal with the awkward Yank, Jones. He behaved like a spoilt child. He had bought some food from someone who wasn't even on our strength and it had been suspect. As a result, he had been ill and somehow seemed to think it was all my entire fault!

The International Y.M.C.A., God bless them, sent some books, games and musical instruments. We celebrated with an impromptu concert in the Officers' billet and Tenko was delayed until eight o'clock.

There was no Christian celebration for Easter that year but the time was memorable because the cherry blossom was in full flower and the mountain sides looked beautiful. Other wild flowers were in bloom and I picked bunches of flowers to place in the billets and cheer them up. The Japanese called the flowers Yamabuki. To me, they were just yellow flowers, like long sprays of lily of the valley, but they were cheerful and colourful.

On the Wednesday of Easter week, we received an issue of corned beef and pears because it was the Emperor's birthday. If that was what was needed to make them open the Red Cross parcels, they could have as many national holidays as they liked. The men were issued with five cigarettes each and, for some unknown reason, two Angora rabbits arrived. They became pets. One of the new guards who had arrived at the camp pestered me for my sergeant's chevrons and the eagle from my R.A.F. jacket. Eventually I gave them to him with great reluctance. In return, he gave me 90 cigarettes, a jack knife and a tin of caramels.

May started with Jones deciding not to number off at Tenko. This earned him a bashing from the guard and he and all the members of his hut were made to stand to attention for a full hour. That might not sound very much but the men were tired after a day's work. They were hungry and most of them were weak.

My mate Les Fulluck returned to work on May 15th. He looked and felt much better. That evening, I was detailed for a firewood fatigue to supply the Commandant's house. This gave me the chance to walk through the village and look at the gardens and the wooden houses. The weather was much warmer now and we talked as we loaded the trucks. Things seemed more relaxed. There seemed to be a lot of fish in the river and the Nips spent a lot of their time fishing and the boys swam.

The first week of June was declared Green Cross week. I thought that must be similar to the Red Cross and perhaps their supplies would be released to us at last. Flags were flying. We didn't see the extra rations though, in fact our rice rations were cut.

Squadron Leader Grant received a letter that week. It had been posted the previous October. If only I could have been so lucky. The following week, some more letters were distributed but there was still nothing for me. I got on well with the Squadron Leader. He was one of the officers who would take time to talk to us and show concern about the men. It was the same for the officers as well as the men in that the conditions we found ourselves in brought out both the best and the worst of their characters. The officers were not required to work as the rest of us were and tended to keep themselves to themselves. Squadron Leader Grant was different. He always showed a great interest in the men's welfare and tried to stand up for them. He was concerned about the men in ESO on one occasion and went out and fed them with his own rice ration. The CO released the prisoners soon after that.

Les's leg suddenly became swollen and ulcerated. He was excused working because they were so bad. Several of the men were suffering with ulcers. Those of us who did go to work had to stand to pay respect to a Japanese Admiral who had been killed in action off the Aleutian Islands. When we got back to camp that evening, I discovered I had been appointed skivvy of the day for the Japs. That meant I had the privilege of washing their dishes, cleaning the tables and sweeping the floors and passages and cleaning Mushymouth's office, his bath and wooden accessories and polishing his light copper kettle in which he boiled the water for his tea.

While we were working, we would hear the sirens going back at the camp four or five times a day. We had no idea why but presumed they were celebrating something, probably the fall of Singapore that had happened eighteen months previously.

A smiling Japanese sergeant, (they always smiled when they wanted to say something unpleasant), told Squadron Leaders Blanchard and Grant that they must stand with their heels together when at attention at Tenko. Blanchard remarked quietly, "Tell him arseholes from me". As if in support of him, another American officer, Lt. Colonel Faulkner gave out the order, 'Sugary,' to dismiss the men rather than the Japanese command, 'Owari' which means finish. The lads really appreciated this. It was quite a change finding the officers making some kind of protest. The Japs didn't respond.

The temperature reached 92 degrees Fahrenheit by noon that month. Working on the stone crushing gang was hot work. The concrete mixer was at the upper level and the stone crusher was near it. We had to crush the larger stones so that they could be mixed with the concrete. It was a dusty, dirty, hot job that gave me a really hard day but it gave each of us a packet of brown tobacco, horsehair we called it. Takashima, the Nip in charge, presented it to us. It was the first time he had ever given us anything so it was a bit more special. Although some of us didn't have much use for it, it was something else with which to barter.

After that, I had a new job, loading cars that fed the concrete mixer. We were sited some 250 metres higher up the slopes, well away from the digging. The scenery was exceptional and it was so quiet and peaceful, an ideal spot for prayer and reflection. When we got back to camp, we were each issued with a tin of beef and some pears, probably Red Cross supplies that had been hidden from us for so long. I was surprised that the pears were still in good condition.

I got on well with the Korean hanchos and hoped that I would eventually be able to buy food from them. Meanwhile they changed a ten yen note for me and that was a great help. Our medical sergeant, Shichino San was also well liked. He worked hard with the sick. We were sad to hear that he was leaving us. In his farewell speech he said,

'Now that I must leave here and part with you all, I recall deeply the happenings of the past six months. I am very glad that the condition of health of all prisoners has improved. I have noticed that the conditions in the work place have improved noticeably. I think this is due to the fact that the weather is better than when you first came here and also that each one of you has been careful of your health, working diligently and keeping yourselves clean. I hope that in the future, you all will take good care of your health and keep yourselves in the proper frame of mind. If you feel that you might become ill you should consult the doctor promptly and receive proper medical treatment and follow the instructions of the medical orderlies. In closing, I pray that God may bless the souls of the deceased and that He will bless the health and happiness of each of you. These are my farewell words to all of you.

He left amid cheers from most of us and he was accompanied to the station by the officers and three of the orderlies. He had certainly been popular but the moment was spoiled by one of the Jap sergeants punching Simple Simon and shutting him in the guard room without any clothes. It didn't concern us but we didn't like it. Simple Simon was harmless. He had been invalided out of the Japanese army and was a guard at the camp.

The Japs didn't seem concerned about him at all and, three days later, he was still in the guard room, presumably still without clothes.

The river was in full flood and flowing fast. One of the Koreans was knocked into the water by a cable and there wasn't a hope of rescuing him. We worked on the dam shelf. It was pleasant up there but very hot and one of the Koreans and an STC lad took the opportunity to swim in the flooded pit. The warm weather brought new problems, flies and ants and they all seemed to be attracted to my bed space.

I was getting really fed up with the bickering between the Yanks and the STC lads. I handed over leadership of the section to Pratt, one of the Americans. Groves, Jones and Mitchell joined in with the Yanks, and started to accuse the lads of stealing curry and soap. What a mentality. What an argument ensued. Later, Groves, the trouble maker, was given the job of rice server and that didn't please him either.

It was announced that eight of our officers were leaving to go to the officers' camp in Tokyo and Mushymouth asked for someone to make a speech of farewell to them. I stood up and wished them luck and a quick return home at which Mushymouth shouted out, 'No, no'. I replied with, 'Yes, yes' and left it at that. Perhaps it was because the officers had left and there were fewer mouths to feed, but the food improved for a short while. Squadron Leader Grant had given me a sarong before he left and it proved to be one of the most useful garments I had.

A few days later, Mushymouth left the camp and the Koreans took over the work site. Our new interpreter was very helpful thank goodness. We couldn't have coped with another Mushymouth.

The food improved marginally although it was never enough. Then we discovered that the officers had Red Cross foodstuffs in their billets. Perhaps that was why they weren't arguing for better rations for the men. Korillis fainted as we were preparing for early morning Tenko. I thought he had died but fortunately he hadn't and he was soon back on his feet. What he needed was proper nourishment as we all did.

Lethargy set in with the colder weather. We knew that we had to keep warm in the months ahead and wondered if the clothes that had been confiscated would be returned to us. When Christmas Eve, our second in captivity, arrived, the Japanese saw fit to inform us what they believed were the five precepts for all prisoners.

1. We are thankful for the just treatment accorded us by the greater Nipponese Empire and we will fulfil our duty to work.
2. We have fulfilled our duties to our respective countries and we have hope for the future.
3. Our complaints and dissatisfaction will make our lives more difficult and will make us lose our hope.
4. We will conquer all hardships and illness for the sake of realising our hope that we will lead an honourable way of life.
5. We will uphold all orders and regulations and we pray for a pleasant and honest life.

And there we had it, straight from the dragon's mouth. I couldn't understand why they thought it was necessary to come up with such nonsense. I found it embarrassing.

Christmas Day was another forgettable work day. There were no celebrations to welcome in the year of 1944. The Second World War had taken precedence. One miserable day followed another miserable day where the bitter cold and poor diet dominated our thoughts and this was tinged with disappointment. There had been another delivery of letters and still there was nothing from home. I was sure that my Joyce would have written to me. Then, to add to our misery, the water pump packed up. Fortunately I was able to repair it and get it working again. At the same time I was made aware that American Red Cross parcels had been delivered to the camp. They were distributed on the January 28th at the rate of two parcels between three men. We had a glorious afternoon dividing the contents. I shared mine with Bert Train and Frank Smith. We had a fire all day. It was a real bonus day. The butter was really creamy and the cigarettes were typically American and full size. But, to our disgust, all the tins of powdered milk had been withdrawn.

The acting officer commanding (O.C.) at that stage was a sergeant and he seemed to be a good natured and considerate chap. The atmosphere was more relaxed altogether but there was still a lot of sickness among the lads and I wasn't the only one that still seemed to be losing weight, not that I thought I had any more weight to lose.

But something seemed to be going wrong. There was no information circulating in the camp. We did not know what was happening in the war. We began to feel that we were cut off from the rest of the world, that we had been forgotten.

I was still enjoying the contents of the Red Cross parcels during the first week in February and we had been allowed to keep the fires burning in the huts. I'd been able to enjoy toast, butter, cheese, grape jam, soup and pumpkin with gravy followed by a very rare cup of coffee and I still had some prunes, beef and spam left. On top of that, some books had been delivered to the camp and I was able to indulge in my favourite past-time, reading.

The visiting Colonel's inspection that Tuesday morning went without incident but he had another mission to perform. He interviewed all the STC lads those that were left, for they had suffered several deaths. He tried to persuade them to change to the Japanese side and join the Chandra Bose army. Not one of them agreed to go. Despite all the fights and battles we had had with them, they stayed firmly on our side. The Colonel was obviously disappointed but he didn't take it out on them. It didn't prevent him giving us extra rations that day. In addition to that, we were issued with bonus tickets which we had to purchase at 5 sen each. We hadn't any idea what these bonus tickets were for but we gathered it was a great honour for us to have them.

Four days later, on February 12th, I collapsed without warning. I was running a high fever and had excruciating chest pains. Fortunately the guard had the presence of mind to call the doctor and I was moved to the sick quarters. I had a serious attack of influenza bordering on pneumonia. I can't ever remember feeling so ill. Then, two days later, our doctor, Lieutenant Whitfield, was moved to another hospital. We were told it would only be for three weeks but there had been a serious outbreak of pneumonia and he was needed at another camp. That was just my luck.

The following day, I was issued with twelve oranges and the next day I received another fifteen. They were obviously trying to pump me full of vitamin C. It was a good job I liked oranges and I got stuck into them and the enterprising orderlies made marmalade from the skins. The rest of my diet was a ladle of 'Ima Kusa' (a type of porridge) morning, noon and night. I was also given half a loaf of bread (a Japanese loaf being little bigger than a bread roll) and promised the second half the next day. For a drink, I was given milk that had been mixed up from the dried milk that had been in the Red Cross parcels. I had resented it being taken out of the parcels at the time but I appreciated it now. Only three of us received that milk. We had half a mug in the morning and another in the afternoon.

Thankfully the pain in my chest eased but it was replaced by a slight, annoying cough. By this time there were seventeen patients in the sick bay and the need for a doctor had risen alarmingly. We were banned from eating all food except for four spoonfuls of the milk mixture twice a day. Fortunately my pal Les came to the rescue and managed to obtain an egg and that helped to stay the hunger pains.

I began to feel better but I couldn't sleep and, when I did, I experienced dreams close to nightmares. I was given some trianon tablets which the officers had managed to get hold of. I didn't know what they were for and I don't think they did either but I took them. In a desperate situation you take anything that is offered. Despite the hunger and the cold, - it was snowing heavily outside - I improved slowly. We were issued with an extra shirt because of the drop in temperature and that was appreciated.

At the end of that week, the Nip doctor gave me a thorough examination. He said that the pneumonia had cleared but I was still showing signs of influenza and pleurisy. Suddenly, I didn't feel quite as well as I thought I did especially as I was to stay on the same diet. That was the day my first boil appeared. A lot of men at the camp had been suffering from boils. The temperature didn't help my frame of mind either. It had dropped to 17 degrees below freezing. It made me want to get up and move about just to keep warm. But I was feeling weak and the lack of solid food didn't help. Even the little we had been having was now stopped and replaced with small amounts of white rice and a little Jap stew. We did however have half a small loaf and, once again, Les came to the rescue. He managed to get some pumpkin and sugar which he converted to jam which we had on our bread. I don't know he managed that but it was a life saver. My feet had begun to swell up and I really thought I was suffering from beri-beri.

There were only five of us left in the sick bay. The twelve that had left had all walked out on their own two feet. Death, thank goodness, had taken a holiday.

I had developed a bout of diarrhoea which was all I wanted. I was treated with injections of vitamin B to deal with my swelling feet. The temperature outside still seemed to be dropping. We were issued with another shirt and a pair of pants but we were still not allowed to light fires in the huts. But we were given ten cigarettes apiece and I received my pay, 1 yen 40 sen from which ten sen had been deducted for baiting. I never did find out what they were baiting.

I was feeling despondent and I decided to do what I had always done and still do when I feel depressed and that was to write everything that I felt down on paper. That way I get it off my mind.

I was discharged from the sick quarters on the last day of February after injections of vitamins C and B. The month had passed in a blur and I can't say I felt well at the end of it. It was as if the time had disappeared from my life. I returned to the same conditions, the same lack of news from the outside world and still no letter from home. Perhaps I wasn't praying hard enough. The one good thing was that I was able to soak in a long hot bath before Tenko that day and that helped a lot. The meal didn't though. The rice was burnt yet again.

I had light duties for the next three days and I was assigned to the tea shack with the task of brewing tea for everyone. This was a kind gesture because it meant I could sit close to the fire and the heat from it proved more beneficial than any of the other treatment. March 6th was a rest day and I was able to soak in another hot bath. It all helped.

March 8th was the anniversary of our capitulation. I thought with longing of the warmth of that day. It was still bitterly cold at the camp particularly at night. You could never get away from the cold. It was always with you. I had another day at the tea shack and then I was U.O.D. again. Thankfully that was the day I received four pears for ten sen and a good day's share of the rations. There were plenty of daigons that day and I was lucky enough to get some extra from Dunlop. But on March 10th I was back at work on the stone crusher in the quarry. I was still very weak but the day was made more pleasant because the sun was getting warmer. We returned to the camp at 1515 hours and I was able to soak in another hot bath. That was the day we received an issue of bread that had been made outside the camp and it was delicious. That evening our meal comprised grey gravy with daigons and we were able to soak up the gravy with bread, - just like being at home.

I was working in the tunnel that was being constructed as part of the dam when I was hit on the head. It was a dangerous job and I was determined to get away from it as soon as I could. But, whether it was the bang on the head or a recurrence of the old problem, I don't know but I suffered chest and neck pains again and started to feel worried and depressed.

That was alleviated when I was issued with a Red Cross handkerchief. It seems ridiculous now to think of the pleasure that gave me but when you were living in the conditions that we were, little things meant so much. By Monday, my pains had eased but I still felt depressed. Even a hot bath didn't help to lift my spirits. Had I been at home, I would have been able to sort myself out but after two years in captivity, not knowing when it was going to end or how my family at home were faring meant that it was only too easy to fall into such a state.

Then we were issued with pullovers that had been supplied by the Red Cross. That was followed by a pair of socks each and a pair of pyjamas. What a difference they made to a good night's sleep. The following day we had a wonderful Red Cross blanket each, not one of the cardboard ones that the Japs used, and a sweater.

I was back on light duties again and managed the tea shack. The only drawback was that I missed the men's company. Despite extra rations of rice, vegetables, stew and some reasonably fresh bread, I was pleased that Sunday, March 26th was declared a rest day. It was also pay day and I received 2 yen 10 sen for two weeks work. And so we drew to the end of March, another month with no letters from home but supplies of warm

Part of an actual cement bag used to build the dam

70

clothing courtesy of the Red Cross.

April showers came early that year and stayed with us during the first few days of April. By this time our work on the dam was almost finished and the atmosphere was more relaxed. Doctor Whitfield returned to the camp to find there were only five patients in sick quarters. Easter Sunday was a rest day and there were letters for some of the lads but still nothing for me. We held a service and sang the hymns that we had been practising and I spent the afternoon designing an Easter card for Bert Train in which I wrote,

'This day I wish you happiness
As much as can be found
For though away from those you love
Their faith is ever sound.
Be strong, be true, be ever bright
For soon you will be free
And then true happiness you'll find
As you would have it be.
WCR

At the end of the week, 98 of us were changed to another billet. We were then told to return our footwear and working clothes. That was a strange and unexpected thing to do and left most of us puzzled until Captain Hewitt gave us the reason. We were moving out at 0500 hours the next morning. There was no mention of where we were going but we were all gripped with such a sense of excitement that anyone would have thought we were going home. In the afternoon, we had to take all our kit to the parade ground and have it inspected. Then we were issued with working pants and a jacket, all of which were ridiculously small. The Japs never did work out that Yanks and Europeans were larger than they were. We got to wear Red Cross boots at last and were also issued with a tin of corned beef each and a packet of Kraft cheese which we had to share between two men. 50 tins of powdered milk were issued to take with us and we each received three blankets. One blanket was sent on ahead, the other two were for use at night.

Chapter Six
Kinose & Carbide Furnaces

Sunday April 16th, started very early for us. We were woken at 0230 hours. Breakfast was at 0300 hours. Tenko was at 0500 hours and we were at the station an hour later. 140 of us were on the move and we were all crammed into one carriage with our kit. We passed through Matsumoto, Kashiwazaki and over a high range of snow clad mountains, during which we changed trains five times and finally arrived at our destination at 2125 hours.

Our first sight of our destination was not encouraging. The works was a carbide and carbon producing factory. Shafts of red and orange light pierced the night sky. The whole area looked foreboding and it didn't help that we had to be guided down mountain paths when we left the station, our way lit by paper lanterns.

We reached the camp at 2200 hours where we were given hot water, rice and stew with miso, a bean paste, and a slice of ginger before getting under our blankets at midnight. We were exhausted. We had been travelling for sixteen hours and when I lay down, I felt as though I was still travelling on the train, the ground still seemed to be on the move.

As we were leaving for the station an STC had handed me a note which read.

'Boys we are all men fighting for the same cause. We have been through a pretty tough time together both on the boat coming over to Japan and during our stay in the camp.

We STC, ever since our capture, have experienced a shortage of NCOs but because of the kindness and understanding of both the Britishers and Americans we have pulled through so far with only three casualties. Now that you are all leaving us, we STC as a whole wish to thank you from the bottom of our hearts for the guidance, understanding and kindness you have shown us. Quarrels and scraps might have been caused by slight misunderstandings but let us forget them all and part as friends.

We are sorry we can only express our gratitude by words because of present rugged days but there will come a time when we Malayan boys might be able to do something. So until that time, we wish you all a pleasant journey and all the luck there is. So three cheers for the Yanks and the Britishers.'

And to think of all the trouble they had caused me!

There was some delay before we started work because the Colonel from Tokyo wanted to speak to us. He informed us that our new camp was referred to as N° 16 Detached Camp and we would be working at the carbide furnaces of the Kanose P.O.W. Camp. He told us that 100,000 letters, books and pencils had arrived at Tokyo earlier that month and that a Sergeant Ochaito had been nominated as the interpreter of N° 1 Camp and Kuriyama San would be the interpreter at ours. By then, it was 1415 hours and a meal of rice with beans mixed in it, pickled radish, carrots and miso paste had just been served up. We were ravenous by then. At the same time, a similar mixture was issued which had to be picked up and taken to work with us for the meal during the break at 2000 hours.

Fortunately both meals had been liberally covered with flavouring, mainly pepper and tongarashi, a mixture of curry and fish powder. Was it hot! It was a mixture that was often used to disguise the flavour of the food.

The bell sounded at 1540 hours and we assembled on the parade ground having first picked up our food, water bottles and anything else we thought we might need. Then we were put through ten minutes of Taiso or P.T. directed by an over enthusiastic instructor. It was not popular especially as he seemed to be bubbling over with energy and we were all feeling extremely tired.

We then moved off to the works where we went through another Tenko and then had to salute the works' manager. Then we were assigned to the different furnaces. There were four men at each one but six were sent to the larger N° 8 furnace. The lads we replaced were more than pleased to hand over to us. Eight hours in that heat had been as much as they could stand. The Nips had considered introducing twelve hour shifts but fortunately they gave that idea up.

The first thing we did was to take off our jackets and shirts and wrap towels round our faces so that we looked like a group of surgeons rather than foundry workers. If the fires weren't in immediate need of attention, we would throw our clothes into the water tank, ready to be washed during firing periods. They soon dried out in that heat.

There were three fires to each furnace and the first thing we did was to find out who was the hancho in charge of the various fires. We soon learned which answer deserved a grimace or a thumbs up.

When the factory furnace San Ban (San = three, Ban = number) blew we headed for the fuel pile along with the hancho. The fuel was a mixture of Siki, (limestone rock), and tan, (coke, coal or carbon). The heat thrown out by those fires was debilitating and, in no time at all, we would all be oozing perspiration from tip to toe. I drank twelve pints of liquid on each shift and I needed it. The barrow boys who were responsible for keeping the stokers supplied with gingo, (fuel), were kept busy. They had to make sure the mixture was right. Too much siki made the carbon electrode fall too low and too much tan caused it to rise too high.

The blowing of the fire happened with unfailing regularity and usually took ten minutes to load it enough to subdue it. Then we would have a few more minutes to sort out our dhobi. We soon learned to ignore the dust and the fumes.

The hanchos changed duties at 1800 hours and the Nipponese crews at 1900. That was the signal for the lads to start warming up the food they had brought ready for their break at 2000 hours. Some were able to use an electric fire but most of us used a spadeful of hot carbide which was enough to give the food some warmth. Tea was also brewed in the same way and those of us who had hung on to our issue water bottles were pleased that we had. We were allowed a thirty minute break and this gave us time to have our meal and a quick smoke, if we had a cigarette that is. That meal break was a real life saver. As men arrived at each changeover, they quoted the time and that seemed to make the shift go faster.

The roar of the fires and the deafening hum of the extraction plant, the dust, fumes and glare of the fires was my idea of 'Hades'. It was hell on earth. There was additional noise from the electric motors that were needed to produce hydraulic pressure on the carbon loaded electrodes which were cooled in turn by water jackets. The electrodes slowly descended into the furnace. Then damn! San Ban, N° 3, blew like hell again before it was expected, leaving a huge hole to be filled yet again and a gong was sounding. This indicated that three men had to go below to assist in pulling away the 'nabe' of molten carbide to the building opposite. The yellow glare and resulting shower of sparks of the molten carbide as it gushed

Aerial view of the Kanose Carbide Works

into the 'nabe' from the bottom of the furnace would have dwarfed any firework display.

The 'nabe'was a small trolley on which all the molten waste and slag was loaded. It was set on rails beneath the furnace and the glare and sparks illuminated the surrounding area in a brilliant, dazzling light. When an empty 'nabe' was pushed against the full obe, there was another shower of sparks as there was when the hancho pushed a hole through the crust in order to take a sample for testing and analysis. Extreme care had to be taken to avoid being burned. Special rag gloves were issued to protect our hands but we had to be careful that they weren't badly worn. Each man had to check that himself. The hancho was a good type though and he looked after the men's requirements. He was a man from the local village.

Once the men had removed three or four of these 'nabes', they would return to the resting place upstairs and help themselves to a drink of hot water or tea. An enormous quantity of liquid was consumed during each shift. All water had to be boiled and salt was issued to replace the salt we lost through sweating. It was a fantastic relief to sit outside between firing periods and feel the cool night breeze on one's skin. N° 2 shift had that advantage over N° 1 shift who had to work during the heat of the day. Then San Ban blew yet again. This time we had to use a rake to push the pile of accumulated gingo around the carbon core and that brought the man who was operating the rake even closer to the searing heat. Goggles were not in common use at that time and the sparks could result in an eyeful of carbon dust. This would be removed with a piece of bamboo. Bamboo was used for all sorts of things. Another hot job was having to tighten the carbon electrode water jacket.

Most of the Nipponese workers were ex servicemen and it was obvious why many of them weren't fighting. Perhaps they would have missing fingers or would show some sign of ill health. It was hard to understand how they managed to cope with the work but they did, usually on the most meagre food rations of plain white rice with fish or whale blubber or, occasionally an egg. Eggs, fats and sugar were extremely rare.

When it was time to hand over to Nº 3 shift, we would fill up our water bottles with hot tea to take back to camp but, first of all, we would have to stoke up the fires. Then we would really wrap up before we made for the bath house. It always felt cold after experiencing that extreme heat.

That communal bath was a wonderful tonic for all of us. We would rid ourselves of all traces of sweat, grime and carbide and sing our heads off. We would then amble across to the camp and another Tenko outside the guard room before making our weary way to our billets by the light of the glare from the furnaces. The orderlies would have collected the buckets of soup and rice and we would settle down to the last meal of the long and tedious day before settling down beneath our blankets.

It took a little time for the routine to become established and, at first, it rained continuously. Working outside was really miserable. Our first hancho was a domineering type who insisted we didn't let up whatever the weather. He even made us eat our meal while we were on the job. But we managed to get plenty of rest because the machinery broke down. The main grouse was, as always, about the food, both the quality and the quantity. There was a slight improvement though as soon as our own cookhouse was in operation run by Sammy and Quennel and overseen by a Nip hancho. Conditions were better than those we had experienced at the quarry. Two officers had transferred with us, Captain Hewitt, an American and Flight Lieutenant Chater of the Canadian Airforce. We could not have had better. Only two of the STC lads came with us and, sadly, we were unable to discover what had happened to the others.

The one big drawback was the rain, the continuous rain, and the Red Cross boots with which we had been issued were not much use in the wet conditions. I managed to grease mine and that helped. The camp itself was commanded by a young lieutenant who was a considerate type. Latrines were much better than at the previous camp and men were given two cigarettes each shift. Things were looking up.

May came in as a beautiful summer's day which put most of the lads into a more relaxed mood but it made me feel really nostalgic and I couldn't get thoughts of home and an English spring out of my mind. That Friday, I refused to accept the Kimari (work schedule) for that day. They were expecting the men to work far too hard. I did win a reduction to ten trucks per day but it meant that I was not the most popular man on the camp. I was reassigned to the N°. 4 furnace, the most difficult furnace to keep in check. As it happened it wasn't a bad day to get stuck indoors because it was bucketing down with rain yet again and at least I was in the dry. It was still tiring work but it was my lucky day because when I got back to the billet, Captain Hewitt yelled out, "Come and get your mail, Rose."

Did I move. I was handed two letters and I stood there for a few seconds holding them in my hand, two letters from home. It was like a great weight being lifted from my mind. One was from my family in Catford and the other was from my Joyce and Malcolm - I had a son. I felt like a real Dad at last. I had a two year old son and I had no idea what he looked like. I longed for a photo of him. I wanted to know all about him.

The letters had been posted in October and November, 1943 *(See page 127)*. They had taken over six months to reach me. I was so thrilled to have them that I couldn't resist reading and rereading them. It was like having a tonic. I felt on such a high that I started telling the lads how much they had to live for. I think the whole camp knew I had a son. I couldn't keep that news to myself. I didn't even mind going back to that dreadful furnace but I didn't have to. I was back at my old job. I got on well with the boss of the N°1 furnace. The shifts had changed so that we were working twelve hours and then having twenty four off. At least we were able to have a whole day off between shifts. A few days later, there was another post and I received three more wonderful letters, two from my Joyce and another one from Catford.

We had an issue of bread that day and we only had to work an eight hour shift. Things were getting better. Then we had another two issues of bread on the Friday and, to add to that, we saw a delivery of Red Cross parcels arriving as we set off for work. The C.O, distributed them straight away and we had a great time sharing out a parcel between five men. My share comprised pork loaf, one and two fifths tins of butter, a twelve ounce tin of meat, 4 squares of chocolate, 2 packets of soup powder, one fifth of a tin of milk powder, 30 cubes of sugar, 12 prunes, a tablet of soap, two fifths of a packet of cheese and one fifth of a packet of raisins and 72 cigarettes, manna indeed. I don't think anyone who hasn't experienced extreme deprivation, can appreciate how much these parcels meant to us. It wasn't only the food although, God knows, we needed these extras but it also meant that people back home knew where we were and understood. They really were life savers.

Then on the following Monday, we were paid for two weeks work. I received the princely sum of 2 yen 30 sens. So I made my way to the canteen and bought black tea, cocoa and fish powder. The so called cocoa was only a substitute for the real thing but it was another extra.

Just when I was feeling happier, I developed a boil on my knee and swelling in my groin. In addition to that I developed a cold and suffered pains in my chest. I felt so unwell that I reported sick at nine o'clock the next morning. Bert Cowell, the medical orderly massaged my chest with some Japanese wintergreen ointment. Then the boil burst and the swelling in my groin went down. That made life a bit easier except that I had broken my molar and exposed the nerve and it was giving me gyp. Then I broke one of my bottom teeth. It was my own fault. I'd been trying to crack a prune stone.

I was back at work by this time and I was finding the work really tiring and the furnaces exceptionally hot. I wasn't good for anything except getting under my blanket at the end of the shift. Our meals were ample and they needed to be to allow us to do the work, but it wasn't the food we would have chosen. We ate what we were given and were pleased to have it. Memories of the hunger back at the quarry were still with us. Unfortunately the bread supplies had stopped because they were doing construction work in the kitchens. We were fed whale meat, bones mostly. I wouldn't have dreamed of eating such a thing back home but we ate it and I won't say we enjoyed it but it satisfied us. We had a lot of greasy soup as well.

Friday, May 19th was my son's birthday. I knew that now and I wondered how he and Joyce were spending the day. I couldn't wait until I was able to share his birthday with him. A week later, I received another letter from Joyce. This was dated 29.5.43. and had obviously been sent before the ones I had already received. Nevertheless, it gave me a lot of pleasure and I read and reread it over and over again.

May turned into June with not a lot going for it. I had been helping lay the concrete for pig stys and had been rewarded with some bread and an issue of sugar, two spoonfuls, but then sugar was very short in Japan. Now I spent time building a goat pen and rabbit hutches. This work was being done on my days off from working at the furnaces. It brought rewards, I was given extra treats of food, all of which were welcome.

The C.O. came round and questioned us at work. Do you like the work? Are you learning about it? Are you the hancho? We answered, 'Yes', to all three and that seemed to satisfy him. From then on we received a daily issue of salt and the pond was stocked with fish. I wasn't sure what kind of fish they were but they reminded me of catfish. The rabbits had arrived and I had to make two more hutches. I was also required to make a ping pong table for the C.O. and I did some more work on the bagatelle board I was making for the lads. I was really busy but it was work I enjoyed doing and I received extra food for my efforts. I still had my daily shift to do at the furnace. We were given an extra towel each to protect our faces and we were also given green tea and rock salt. The Hancho gave each of us in his group a dungo. It was made from red beans and, despite its name, it tasted particularly good.

There was another C.O.'s inspection later that month and he was obviously pleased with us because we were each rewarded with an apple. June 7th was a memorable day. The first was that we were inoculated against typhoid in our left breast. This was repeated five days later. Because of this we were not allowed to have a bath after work. Secondly, the news came through that Europe had been invaded. Through clandestine means we got to hear about it and we prayed that this was not another piece of 'duffgen' and that if they had landed, it wouldn't turn out to be another Dunkirk.

A week later we were taken by surprise by the arrival of a RAMC doctor and an American M.O. from Tokyo. They brought the optimistic news that the end of the European war was in sight. They also informed us that we would be having our own British M.O. from Hong Kong in the next few weeks. That was good news. We were feeling much happier when we went for our meal, octopus tentacles, - we were living in strange times. The meal also had its share of tough fish, bamboo shoots, digon, turnip, rice, beans and potatoes, all in a soup.

Later that week, I built a bridge over the fish pond and completed some jobs for the cook. He always paid me with extra food. The weather was glorious and the countryside looked wonderful. How I wished I could be back in the garden of England and enjoy the summer there. We were all getting brown from the sun.

A Wop, (an American Italian) passed away that week. His was the first death we had had at the camp. His burial service was held at 1430 hours. His body was placed in a coffin of pine wood and accompanied by a bowl of rice and Tongarashi, a plate of strawberries, a plate of biscuits, two tins containing paper flowers, an American flag, a crucifix and a wooden stand for a black cross. There was also a blue flowered box for burning joss sticks and a box for his ashes placed on a table surrounded by Marguerite rambler roses. The Japanese allowed and showed a lot of respect.

There was a presentation the next morning. I was presented with a 50 sen note for good attendance at the furnace and a packet of tobacco for my work on the rabbit hutches. We were also told that we were going to get an extra ten sen a day for work but, as always happened when something good happened, there was something else to balance it. On this occasion we were told that our rations were going to be cut. A rumour started about this time saying that another 100 P.O.W.s were going to join us. In fact 102 turned up and they were all English. They had been captured at Singapore, Formosa or in the Philippines. They all had a story to tell. They had been brought over to Japan in a hell hole of a boat similar to the one that we had travelled in. Their boat had been sunk one day out from Japan and a lot of men had been lost. Many of these were sick. It was a good job that extra medical help had arrived. It was needed. The new arrivals were soon introduced to the cook's speciality, burnt rice.

As June came to the end we were told that we had a pay increase of 25 sen a day. That brought our fortnightly pay to 3 yen 45 sen. We were also told that we were not to sit on the same seats as the Nip workers on the furnace sites, nor were we to talk to them. That night, the interpreter left the camp.

July followed on without any change except that the C.O. refused to believe that we had followed his orders. He accused us of speaking to the Nip workers at the furnace site and sitting on the same seats. Then he came along the lines and slapped each one of us, - hard. He had seemed a considerate fellow until then, now we saw a different side of him.

This was followed by the sergeant hitting 19 men round the face with a stick. I was one of the nineteen. One of our men hadn't responded to an order quickly enough. He had been carrying a sack of rice at the time. He was knocked to the ground with a bigger stick. Then the sergeant apologised for including me but said he couldn't differentiate. Later that day, I was slapped on the face again with a stick by the same sergeant. My crime that time was that I had spoken while carrying sacks of rice to the cookhouse. The 'powers that be' were not in a good mood. Perhaps they were not happy about the state of affairs in Europe. We had heard that the allied invasion had been successful and our troops were advancing on all fronts.

The cook hancho was very benevolent towards me. I did a lot of odd jobs for him and he always rewarded me with some of his delicacy, burnt rice. I don't know how I would have survived without his kindness. One day, back in the billet, the men started commenting that I was getting fatter. I didn't answer. I wasn't sure if there was spite in their observation. They also commented on the cabbages that I had planted out. I had invited them to give me a hand but they didn't seem keen. It would be a different matter when they were ready to eat. I liked doing the odd jobs around the camp. There was plenty that needed doing and it kept my mind occupied.

It was about this time that the billets were reorganised. The Yanks had to be housed in billets on their own. The orders had evidently come from Tokyo. This was followed by another one of the Nip presentation ceremonies. For my 'good work' around the camp, constructing the animal pens and building the steps to the cookhouse, I was awarded 50 sen, 20 hollow point cigarettes and a 30 sen box of pepper. This pepper, I must add, was not like the pepper we had back in England, this added flavour to the meal. In addition to this, my friend the hancho cook gave me another issue of burnt rice and there was also an issue of bread that day. I was well satisfied.

This was followed by one of the heaviest downfalls of rain that we had ever experienced. It was so heavy that the furnace area was flooded. It was difficult to work in those conditions but we had to get used to it because the rain continued to bucket down for days. The Nips waited until it was at its heaviest and then ordered us to carry out an air raid practice (A.R.P.) at work. The air raid sirens had been going pretty regularly, not that we took any notice of them. We carried on working but the Japs were getting jittery.

I found myself back with the Nº 8 furnace crew, clearing up the mess around it. It was hot, humid work. The heat near the furnace was intense. One of the lads fainted from it. The next day, I had to do the same job for no. 1 furnace. I seemed to have become the odd job boy. I earned extra rations for a carpentry job I did. You've guessed it, another helping of burnt rice! Back at camp, I repaired the fresh water pond. For that I was paid with five peaches. The thought of them still makes my mouth water. They were delicious. I had longed for something sweet and they fitted the bill.

July went into August and the glut of cucumbers with which we had been fed was replaced with a glut of potatoes. On the twelfth, Frank Smith and his team of lads, who called themselves the Kanose Follies gave us a show, 'Carbide Capers'. It was great and really lifted the men's spirits. The Sunday service that week was held on the Tuesday evening. It didn't matter when they were held as long as we had one. They had become very important to the men. I know they were to me. I always had been a Christian. I have no doubt that I found solace in my belief in Almighty God and consolation in prayer and my acceptance that his will be done. I endeavoured to live according to the Christian teaching of our Lord Jesus Christ. I tried to meet the day to day difficulties in my mind and to organise Sunday Services at both the camps in Japan. Being a P.O.W. gave me time to think about things and sort them out in my own mind. The experience turned some men against their faith but it only strengthened mine. I was convinced that one day I would be going home to my wife and son and my faith was a part of that belief. It was very important to me.

Another advantage was talking to the men. They had come from all walks of life and there was so much experience and knowledge amongst them. I spent one evening talking to Squadron Leader Grant. He had worked at Kew Gardens before the war and was an expert on trees. I learned a lot from him. Another man taught me a lot about pigs and pig keeping. The odd thing about that time was that there was very little talk about regaining our freedom and I began to wonder if we were accepting these conditions and that the men were giving up hope of seeing their own homes again.

I welcomed in September with another dose of prickly heat rash and was excused duties, but only for the day. The following week my legs were swollen and covered in sores. I was excused duties again and given multi vitamin tablets. Fresh vegetables were not being provided and we lacked the vitamins they gave us. I left sick quarters at the end of September and was able to take the evening services again.

October 1st, 1944 was our sixth wedding anniversary. How I wished Joyce and myself along with our son could have gone out for a nice meal.

Instead here we were stuck miles away from each other, Needless to say, thoughts of them both stayed with me all day. It didn't help that the Nip Toban chose that time to kill and skin a cat. That horrified me. I would never have dreamed of eating cat.

There were still plenty of odd jobs that needed doing round the camp. Using an old gas cape, I made a pair of bellows. There was a book case to make and all sorts of repairs needed at the Doc's billet. I was given 30 sen by 'Whiskers' for making a table that he wanted to give to his wife for a present. I can remember his face but not his name. Then I had to address my skills to trying to repair Frank's false teeth. It was surprising the jobs I was asked to do. There was always plenty of them and, fortunately, there always seemed to be the materials available to complete them. That there was a more difficult thing altogether. I had to learn all the skills as I went along for a lot of this work but I was sure it would stand me in good stead when I got back to Blighty. Who knew, I might even set up in business on my own as an odd job man? I was the unofficial camp carpenter and earned myself extras on many an occasion, mostly food and that was always appreciated. We now always seemed to be hungry. Hunger was a permanent state. We dreamed of fish and chips, egg and bacon and treacle pudding. For breakfast one day we had rice and barley with persimmons. They were very sweet and very squashed but I don't think any of us had ever tasted them before. For supper we were fed locusts. I didn't fancy them but one of the Japs insisted that I tried one. He said they were good and they were. They tasted rather like toffee. I had plenty to eat that evening because most of the others refused to even try them.

Frank Smith staged one of his best performances that month with his version of Cinderella and a Will Hay type school drama. I sang and performed in the first performance. I had never heard the men laugh so much. It did us all good but even when the performance had been put on for their benefit, some of the men refused to show any interest and shut themselves away or went to a quiet corner to play cards.

Christmas was approaching and, once again I started thinking about carols and a Christmas service. A bullock was slaughtered on Christmas Eve. I had never seen such a thing. It wasn't the kind of thing one saw on the streets of Bermondsey. I can't say that I really appreciated the soup that was made from the animal's bones and blood, but it was food and nutrition, so I shut my eyes and swallowed it.

Sunday service was cancelled yet again, just when I thought I had got it all organised. I began to wonder what was happening to us. We were fast becoming a bunch of atheists. We were suffering from a massive dose of apathy. It was depressing to think that those around you had given up, not only their freedom but belief in their Lord too. It was my belief that gave me strength when things were low and I wanted to share this comfort with the rest of them but it took a lot of effort to get their interest. Initially, services had been well attended but only ten men had come to the last service I had taken. It was so disappointing.

There was a shortage of tobacco and that was serious. Smoking gave the lads the comfort which, unfortunately, the services failed to do. We realised how serious the shortage was when we realised the Nips were smoking tea tree bark. Some of the men started drying tea leaves and smoking those. I'd never seen such things smoked before and I considered it demeaning. But, at the next pay parade, there was another issue of tobacco and that brought the smiles back on the men's faces. I had 3 yen and 68 sen, full pay with only 32 sen deducted for pears and an apple.

Heavy rain and cold told us that Christmas was approaching. Fortunately the billets were warmer here than they had been at the quarry. The fires were a great improvement because they didn't smoke like the coal fires had done. Here we burned the carbide nodes. The only problem with them was that they were difficult to light.

Flight Sergeant Whitley had managed to get hold of a photo projector and asked me to repair it. I never thought of asking where he had got it from. Repairing it proved a bit of a trial because the weather was so cold and my hands were so chapped that the end of my fingers were split open. They weren't too much of a problem for carpentry jobs and there were plenty of those, including making clogs.

It was so cold and it rained, how it rained. Yet when it stopped in the afternoon and the sun shone for a short while, it showed up all the autumn colours and the countryside looked beautiful. The lads were still bringing hot carbide nabes back to the billet and that kept the winter chills at bay and allowed us to dry our clothes. But the cold really got to me and I developed a body cold which made my limbs ache almost to the point of despair. All the same, I earned a sweet potato for repairing a table and 'Whiskers' gave me some tobacco when I mended his umbrella for him.

I had to repair the gates to the camp three times and I thought how ironical that was. If we had been in Germany, it would have been an opportunity for us to all walk out, but Japan was different. There would have been nowhere else to go except somewhere else in Japan. A rumour went round that we were being moved out and some more prisoners were coming in but I didn't take any notice. I just carried on repairing the gates.

I still felt ill from the cold and had been taking powders for days to try and settle my stomach. The food we were having didn't help. It was more like pig's swill than food that would provide sustenance for working men. One evening, the Nip cook Hancho took pity on me and gave me his meal. He also gave me lots of tea and that was the first time for days that I only had to go to the latrines once in the night. I had a good night's sleep and that made me feel better. To cap that, there was another batch of letters, two for me, one from Joyce and one from my family in Catford. They'd been posted in February, so things were speeding up a little. They had taken only nine months to reach me.

Christmas was approaching and I organised carol practices but there was no enthusiasm for them that year. In the end I cancelled them altogether when Bill Eaton was the only enthusiast to turn up. But they were enthusiastic enough when Red Cross parcels turned up and we were able to enjoy raisin pudding, hot coffee with buttered toast, jam and cheese. Those parcels were life savers.

Snow continued to fall and, when it wasn't snowing, it was sleeting. It was so cold but, at least, we had the nabes to give us some warmth. I did spare a thought for the poor devils that had replaced us at the quarry and wondered how they would be coping with such intense cold. I was still suffering with my stomach and I couldn't shake off this feeling of apprehension and depression. Perhaps it was the thought of coming to the end of my Red Cross goodies that caused it. The box was almost empty. There was just a little butter, cheese and jam, enough for one more meal. But that night, I dreamed of home and the dream was so real that I woke up really thinking I was back in England. I had dreamed of warm milk and sugar to settle my stomach and remembered Joyce saying, 'Pass the thing'. She seldom told us what the thing was she wanted. I visualised the cakes cooling in her kitchen cupboard and eating real mince pies after Tenko. I tasted those mince pies. Then I woke up - to a real Tenko and no mince pies!

December 15th was a big meal day. There were extra potatoes, dijons, spaghetti, carrots and onions. It came just right because my Red Cross box was completely empty by then. To overcome my depression, I started making Christmas cards for my pals but I gave that up. It only made me feel more homesick than ever.

Unfortunately my time as the camp carpenter came to an abrupt end when I was ordered back to the furnaces. It was so cold. I didn't know that it was possible for a human being to be so cold. We had to push the cold Nabes into the sheds and the cold numbed our brains as well as our bodies. We had to thaw out before we could start work. We were still rehearsing for the Christmas pantomime but we rehearsed in the bathroom because there was a small fire there that gave some semblance of heat. The problem was that we could not escape the intensity of the cold. There were no extra woollen clothes to wear, no billets where the draughts didn't whistle through the gaps in the walls, no extra source of heat. We had to live and work with the cold. We would report to work soaked through. Fortunately we could dry out in front of the furnaces but feet were always the problem. My feet would be soaked through and bitterly cold, so cold that I didn't feel they belonged to me. It was a constant battle to prevent chilblains. Then I was given the task of clearing the snow from the steps of the lime kiln. It was purgatory.

Then we were told that the C.O. had cancelled all Christmas arrangements. He relaxed that later but we still had to work our normal shifts on Christmas Day. We didn't feel like putting the Christmas show on after that. It didn't do anything for our morale when the C. O. took the opportunity to remind us of the Five Precepts of Dai Nippon Gun.

1. We are thankful for the just treatment accorded us by the great Nipponese Empire and we will fulfil our duty to work.

2. We have fulfilled our duty to our respective countries and we have hope for the future.

3. Our complaints and dissatisfaction will make our lives more difficult and we will lose our hope.

4. We will conquer all hardships and illness and for the sake of realising our hopes we will lead an honourable way of life.

5. We will uphold all orders and regulations and we pray for a pleasant and honest life.

ISSUED TO ALL POWS

Christmas Day 1944 was the most miserable day I have ever spent in my life. I had a bath after the Christmas Eve shift and returned to the billet. We weren't even allowed to change the cold Nabes for hot ones. There were no presents or cards to open, yet the thoughts of my loved ones stayed with me all day. I helped get the scenery ready for the show and managed to get in some sleep before the show. My eyes were burning with tiredness. The lads felt it was essential to put on the show regardless of how we felt and I went along with them although I felt a complete Zombie. I was glad I did. It was a complete success and did a lot to help lift everyone's spirits.

The snow of December carried through into January and became the even heavier snows of 1945. I had never seen snow like it. The tracks along which we normally ran the cold nobbies to exchange them for hot ones had become covered with snow. No sooner had we cleared them than they became covered again, either by more snow or drifting in the heavy winds and the winds blew, piercing, penetrating, powerful winds. It was difficult keeping the furnaces working in such vicious conditions. The only one working with any efficiency was the N° 2 monster.

The snow was so deep that it virtually hid the huts and we walked through tunnels of snow. Women and boys were brought in from the village to clear the snow from the roofs. There were fears that the roofs would collapse because of the weight of the snow.

The heavy snow created difficulties for the cook house in that wood was in short supply and, as a consequence, our bread issue was reduced. We had enough problems without rationing being imposed. Then, with heavy overnight frosts, our fresh water supplies ceased. Then, for one whole day, the snow ceased and it was a wonderful, sunny day and, although we were cold and hungry, we couldn't help wondering at the beauty of it all. There were snow capped mountains in the distance and dark pine trees on the slopes. We didn't have long to look at it. We were given the job of dragging stones from the bed of a river tributary which supplied water to the works and camp. We did succeed in improving the water supply but, working in a running river in that temperature left us frozen to the bone and our fingers and toes stiff with the cold. We weren't the only ones to suffer from the dreadful weather conditions. On our way to the river, we passed a number of small bungalows that were completely covered with frozen snow.

I decided that we needed a sledge and, on my next day at camp, I started constructing one. I asked Flt Lt Chater's advice. He was Canadian and if anyone should have known about sledges it should have been him. He helped me design the thing and I spent hours making it. Well he might have been a good officer but he wasn't much good when it came to sledges.

We had to make two trips to the local station to collect 60 kgs. sacks of potatoes and get them back to the camp. This is where the sledge could prove how useful it was. I had made ropes from plaited straw and several men came with us to pull the thing. Unfortunately, Flt. Lt. Chater hadn't taken the load into account when he had advised me on the design. As soon as it was loaded, the sledge settled deeper and deeper into the snow. We had the maximum number of men pulling it and it didn't budge an inch. In the end, the fifty men that had been detailed to pull the sledge, had to carry the sacks back to the camp and that proved an ordeal, almost an impossibility for some. One of the men found his legs disappearing into the snow and the weight of the sack pushed him down further until he was buried almost up to his neck before we got him out. Several others floundered and fell. We were fed potatoes, butter and cheese when we got back to the camp as a reward but we'd have done better with a hot toddy!

It was bitterly cold and snow continued to fall. The snow was so deep that moving between billets and the work was an impossibility. The wood party had difficulty finding the wood piles. The billets were really cold. We were unable to get Nabes back from the works and one small fire between 44 men was very little help. But I even forgot the cold one day because I received another letter from my darling wife. I was beginning to get a little collection of them and every one was precious.

The following days were a mixture of tragedy and dismal failure. A Nip worker was killed when a carbide Nabe that had been dropped from a crane in the stores exploded. We'd worked with this guy and his death saddened us even though he was Japanese. We were allowed Nabes in the billets again and the warmth was wonderful. To escape from the extreme cold for even a short while was a wonderful experience. Then we were told that no more fires were to be lit in the billets. We couldn't even obtain carbon and we had no idea why. Somehow, we managed to get hot Nabes though, I can't remember how but I can remember sitting round and having a good old sing song one evening. The reason was that Nishino San, our one armed guard had returned to the camp. He was a nice chap and we all liked him. But how changed he looked he had lost a great amount of weight, in fact looked very ill, several of us were concerned that he had had a bad time with the authorities. After the sing song, I suddenly had a bilious attack. I reported to the doctor and he said I had gout. I thought it was more likely to be goat because they'd given me some at the cook house and it had been very greasy. Whatever the cause, I was given two days off duties. I appreciated the rest but it was important to keep myself active and I continued with some carpentry work. The Nip sergeant taking the sick parade said I was to carry on as the carpenter and that suited me. Working close to a fire gave me a chance to get over my health problems. Conditions outside were worse than ever and the snow had risen to a height of seven feet. The path to the ablutions was through a tunnel of snow and the basins were covered with ice.

It was while I was working on my tasks that I was told R.A.F. Sergeant Kidder had been slung in the Eso Musho, (Gaol). He had been caught cooking his personal stock of rice. I thought he was a fool to have been caught cooking it but wondered how he had managed to build up a stock of the stuff in the first place. Rice was delivered to the camp in straw sacks containing 60 kgs. Some of the lads had realised that unloading the sacks was a golden opportunity to get some for themselves. They had taken some hollow bamboo, sharpened one end to a point which they slipped into the sack while the other end was slipped into their trousers. When they lifted the sack, the rice flowed down the pipe and down their trouser legs. They had already tied them at the ankles. They managed to get several pounds of the grain that way and cooked it at their own convenience. Unfortunately Kidder had allowed himself to be caught and given the game away. On the Sunday, the Japs gave the camp a full search but they did not find any more rice stealers. The others who had been in on the scheme had had the chance to get their rice hidden.

A thaw set in at the end of January and life became really miserable for a while. We were walking through slush that made our feet and trouser legs permanently wet. The thaw didn't last long. We were only a week into February when the freezing temperatures and snow returned with a vengeance. The winds blew with a blizzard like ferocity.

Two Americans, Big Stoop Kollick and Badder, were made to stand to attention for five hours holding large lumps of ice. I didn't know what they had done to merit such treatment but having to stand like that in those temperatures bordered on sadism in my book.

I was back at work on the furnaces. How I grew to hate them. The same squad of furnace cleaners also had the task of collecting the wood for the cookhouse fires and clearing snow. It was a long, hard day but, nevertheless, I still found time to complete some of my carpentry tasks including sealing the cookhouse windows and that earned me a gift of biscuits and were they welcome. We were on short rations but, this time, we knew the reason why. Someone had stolen food from the cookhouse. This was a heinous crime by all our standards. Everyone was short of food. The Japs may have had a better selection of food but they had very little more than we did in quantity. To steal food was to take away from everyone else. Stealing from your mates was an unforgivable crime. Things were no better in the village. Our interpreter told us how the local people were suffering from hunger.

Sunday services had completely fallen by the wayside. There seemed to be no interest in the Sabbath day. The lads were so dejected that they even began questioning their faith in God and I couldn't answer their doubts. It was very sad.

At the end of the month, a cow and a calf were brought into the warehouse next to our billet. The cow was slaughtered and the calf was left on its own. One of the Light Duties (LD) men fed it occasionally. Then Jimmy Duffy, the cook, found it lying down looking sick and showing no interest in the new day. Jimmy decided something had to be done and he marched off and confronted the C.O. Either the C.O. couldn't understand Jimmy's mixture of Japanese and Cockney accent or he wasn't interested in the calf.

Jimmy told him that he was going to take the calf into the billet to get it warm. he explained that the small cow was plenty sick with diarrhoea and pneumonia. The C.O.'s response was to ask its number. That took Jimmy by surprise. He looked at him for a minute, then acted out what he was trying to explain, putting his two fingers above his head to act as horns and then lying down on the ground with a lot of facial expression. That so impressed the C.O. that he burst out laughing. Meanwhile the Nip toban (tea boy) had fetched the doctor without telling him that his patient was to be a cow. By the evening, the poor beast had been slaughtered and skinned and was providing food for the villagers.

The C.O. was not so amused when dealing with Big Jones, the American. The big Yank went out for his day shift to the furnaces and discovered his job had been changed. He was to carry carbon, a much dirtier job and he was not going to do it. No Sir, he was not going to do it. Big Jones suddenly developed an illness and reported sick. The C.O. appeared sympathetic and granted him ten days rest. Big Jones hit the blankets. That was the day when there was a camp inspection and beans, blubber and rice was found on his shelf. Big Jones was in trouble. The speed with which he started his ten days' rest in gaol was unbelievable. His feet hardly touched the ground between his bed and the eso. He was also restricted to two thirds of the rations and banned from having his next Red Cross parcel. Martindale, another Yank went the same way. He hadn't had any food but the guards had found a bunch of keys on his shelf.

Those two men must have frozen in the eso. It was a wooden cage, five feet by five feet by four. It was extremely cold and a bitter wind was blowing. It couldn't have helped them to hear us singing round a fire. We had been allowed another issue of Nabes.

I was busy making a couple of foot cradles for the sick bay. Doctor Robinson had operated on Jack Howe, grafting skin on to his foot. Despite the lack of supplies, the graft was successful. I never failed to wonder at how the medical team coped with these situations despite the lack of medical supplies. Many prisoners owed their lives to them. The C.O. released a Red Cross parcel to Jack and another one to Bert Train who was suffering from severe jaundice.

Then another American, a man called Jugbutt, was caught stealing a slab of blubber by his own officer, Captain Hewitt. He wasted no time and handed him straight over to the Nip C.O. Jugbutt was tied up to the Administration building and given a sound beating with the C.O.'s stick before being thrown into the eso with the other Yanks. No sentiment was wasted on Jugbutt. There couldn't be if stealing had to be held in check.

March started with a downpour that continued for days. Red Cross clothing was distributed but only to those of good character. Who, we wondered, decided were those of good character. It seemed we had earned ourselves a spy in the camp. We had called one of the Nip guards Spy without realising how apt it was. One of the officers was banged because he was seen eating four meals a day while two of the cooks were reported because they claimed they didn't know anything about this extra 'meal'.

It didn't take a lot to remember that March 8th was the third anniversary of the fall of Java. None of us had ever expected to still be prisoners for this length of time. March 9th was a very bad day for all of us. Four of our lads received serious burns. Jock Foster, Jack Crowdell, Buchan and Rogers received serious burns when the Nabe to which they were attending was not placed immediately under the outlet of the furnace. The molten carbide flowing from the furnace, hit the edge of the Nabe and spilled on to the floor. The floor was deep in carbide dust and, as soon as the red hot, molten carbide hit it, it exploded. The four men had been standing by with rods, ready to take the Nabe away when it was filled and were unable to escape the inferno. They were dreadfully burned. Jack Crowdell was in agony. Foster, Crowdell and Buchan(2) were taken to the Nip hospital accompanied by two orderlies, our doctor and Captain Jarvis who stayed with them. Three days later, we were told that Jock Foster and Buchan had died from their wounds. Their bodies were brought back to camp and preparations made for their burial. I helped to sort out their clothing and effects. It was a miserable task. The burial service was a typical Japanese ceremony. Large artificial flowers, two glasses of milk and two plates of biscuits, two plates of apples, joss sticks and incense were placed around the bodies before the service. The blankets covering the bodies were taken away and they were placed in their coffins. The coffins had to be carried nine miles to the nearest crematorium. Fortunately the weather was kind to us. The coffins were heavy and the journey was extremely slow. The sun shone and we got sun burned even though we passed houses that were still covered in several feet of snow. We crossed the river by ferry. It was an attractive route. We would have enjoyed the day had there not been such a sad reason for it.

Red Cross parcels were distributed on our return. Fifteen of the lads failed to get a parcel but Big Jones got one after all. The Nip sergeant gave it to him. I enjoyed the contents of mine to the full especially as I'd been given extra butter and a tin of salmon in recognition of the work I did in the camp. To make me feel really good, I received another card from my Joyce.

The gourmet Yanks caught a cat that they had found wandering in the camp. They killed, skinned and cooked it. It smelt like rabbit but I didn't fancy it.

Then came the demoralising news that Jack Crowdell had died, the third of the four burns victims to die. He'd fought to stay alive for fifteen days and then he'd lost the battle.

The weather turned warmer with the coming of April. I was having a lot of trouble with my eyes. The heat from the furnace was affecting them and they became very red and sore. I treated them with saline wet packs and fortunately they worked.

Then it was found that the Nip sergeant had been pilfering from the Red Cross parcels. Captain Hewitt was proving to be the most efficient officer in the camp and he requested that the fifteen men who had not received their Red Cross parcels be given them. The C.O. discovered that the Nip sergeant had been keeping them. It was obvious that pilfering was

(2) These three names are sewn in their memory onto the flag on page 132)

becoming commonplace. Needless to say, the sergeant left the camp.

Air raid sirens had been going regularly but we ignored them. Now they seemed to be going even more. Planes were being sighted frequently although they were often little more than vapour trails in the sky. Blackouts were enforced. Rumours ran rife. We heard that the allies were now in Berlin. Why, we wondered weren't they in Tokyo. The C.O. took off for a break in Tokyo armed with loaves of bread that had been made by Frank Smith. He was good at baking bread and was almost as popular for that as for the shows he produced.

Then Tenko was brought forward and we had to do an hour's digging before we had breakfast. We weren't sure what we were digging but it turned out that we were creating a series of zig zag trenches. Then we had to move wood that was needed for the new administration block. This was all before we started a day's work. It didn't help that I lost my job as the camp carpenter at the same time and was replaced by two men. I was annoyed about that but the first job they had to do was construct a new pig pen and they were welcome to that. Even when we finished working at the furnaces, we had to put in another hour building air raid shelters at the camp.

May came in and it was spring. I thought longingly of home and wondered if I would ever see Heather Cottage in all its springtime glory. Red Cross parcels had arrived at the camp but their distribution was delayed.

Then we heard that both Mussolini and Hitler were dead and, a few days later, that the war in Europe was over. We were elated. I started to wear my ring again. It was a symbol of hope. Nothing could dampen our spirits and, when the Red Cross parcels were distributed later that day, the mood in the hut was jubilant.

We had one parcel between two men. The contents were much the same as before. I shared mine with Spider Collins. Captain Hewitt took ten cigarettes from each parcel to compensate nine men who had not received parcels from the previous issue. I only had a few hours sleep because I was woken up and given a cablegram from my beloved Joycie dated 11.4.45. I was deliriously happy as I set off for work on the night shift. The cablegram was so unexpected and so welcome and seemed to bring us closer together.

When I finally got round to trading my Red Cross parcel, I was left with ten cigarettes, a tin of jam, five sticks of gum, a tin of Prem (something like Spam), half a tin of milk, half a tin of bully beef, half a block of cheese, half a box of sugar, a tin of pate, two tins of milk, a tin of coffee, half a box of raisins and a block of chocolate.

We were eating our meal one evening when the sirens went and aeroplanes were heard overhead. Immediately all the lights went out and we had to eat our food in the dark. The aircraft made three circuits over the camp and then flew on. When we went to work the next day, we found that the Nips had had to line up for Tenko before they had been allowed into the shelters by which time the aeroplanes had left the area.

More cablegrams came but unfortunately there were none for me and I felt disappointed. I knew I shouldn't expect to have something on every delivery but I lived in hope.

May 19th was my son's birthday and I hadn't even seen him or had a photograph of him. Needless to say he was in my thoughts all day. He was three years old and I celebrated with an extra ration of rice and what was left of the butter and jam from the Red Cross parcel. But my feeling of homesickness intensified when I received two cards in the post that day, one from my brother Norman and the other from my brother in law Stanley. They had both enlisted and they were both home in England. I felt thankful for them that they hadn't experienced being P.O.W.s but I felt envious.

Life was still a continuous round of work. Monday was our official bath night but we were more independent and bathed on the job, in the works baths. N° 5 furnace continued giving trouble and poured four nobbies on to the floor. Fortunately nobody was hurt but there was a lot of clearing up to do. We still had additional work to do in the camp. One day, we were sent three miles to collect wood for the new building. When we got back, we had to bang on the gate to be allowed back in, which seemed a ridiculous thing for prisoners to do.

There was an underlying feeling of tension building up in the camp. Jock Flynn was thrown into the eso. His crime had been giving gum to some girls on the site. Then Big Jones, the Yank, was in trouble again. He had missed the P.T. parade and was defiant when he was questioned. He earned himself a bashing from Igowa San who used both his fists and a stick. Then Bob Pratt had a nervous breakdown at work and had to be held down by six men. But he suddenly recovered and walked back to the camp when a Nip threw a rope to tie him down.

Then there was a rush to get the lads out on parade which wasn't a popular move and I got the blame for it. Bert Cowell blew his top and struck out at me. It ended with the two of us having a proper fist fight which, fortunately, I won. The news of the fight soon spread round the camp and lots of people came and congratulated me and asked me why I hadn't dealt with him before. Even Captain Hewitt came and shook my hand. He introduced himself first, "My name's Hewitt", he said as if I didn't already know.

Air raid warnings were becoming more frequent and we often saw the vapour trails made by B29s. Post was becoming more frequent although it was often a year out of date but every bit of news from home was welcome.

June started off beautifully. It was a wonderful summer's day. Then problems loomed with the arrival of 100 more men. We had to cram 44 of them into our billet which was over full to start with. We managed to squeeze them in somehow but it wasn't a good situation. Living too close to your neighbours can cause tension and bad tempers and we certainly didn't want that added to our other problems, but there was no other option. The new inmates were Dutch Javanese who had been at Nagasaki, a camp near Tokyo and had worked in the docks and brickyards there. We now had 150 Dutch prisoners at Kanose. They told us all about the bombing by the Americans and the devastation it was causing.

Our meal that day was baby shark and did it hum! The fish we had had earlier had been sun dried so it didn't smell but this issue of shark made up for it.

The Dutch contingent had arrived in time for our show on June 2nd but it was cancelled and so was our rest day. And the reason was that two of the men who were taking part in the show had been held back from work that day so we all had to be punished. There always seemed to be strange decisions made when the C.O. was absent and he was away that day. When the C.O. returned the rest day and the concert were reinstated a few days later. Then my rest day was cancelled once again. This time it was because Head had had a fight with a driver and had bloodied his nose and hurt his wrist. I hadn't been involved but I had been a bystander so I was punished along with the culprits. But two good things happened to balance the bad. I received news from R.J. Rowlands, an old school teacher of mine, and that gave me food for thought and it was pay day. I received 2 yen 75 sen. One yen had been deducted for apples! And, of course, the show helped to lift our spirits. It started with the cast singing, 'Take me back to Dear Old Blighty', and we all joined in at the tops of our voices. This was followed by, 'It's a Long Way to Tipperary,' and, 'Pack up Your Troubles'.

Later that week there was a concert back at the camp. Unfortunately I was on nights and couldn't attend but I understood that the ukulele I had made had really been appreciated. The only thing that marred that week was that I found it necessary to report the Hancho of N° 6 furnace yet again. He had become more of a nuisance than ever. There was no way his behaviour could be tolerated. He was a bully and blamed us for the troubles on N° 6 furnace.

Then on June 6th., we heard the most amazing news. The ultimatum that the Americans had given to the Japanese was due to expire the next day. The days went on and there was no further news. Faces grew longer and longer as the days went by. We even wondered if the news had been duff. We waited and we hoped.

Then word got round that there had been a major outbreak of typhoid in Kanose village. We were warned against drinking unboiled water or uncooked vegetables. The cooks needed those instructions more than we did. We hardly ever saw fresh vegetables.

Air raids were becoming more frequent and we would be holed up in the air raid shelters for ages except when we were at work. We carried on working then. July started with a midnight air raid. Immediately all the lights were switched off. Looking for our kits and blankets in the pitch dark was almost an impossibility.

The lads had been ordered to plant sweet potatoes in the vegetable patch. Two days later, it was discovered that they had all been stolen. The Nip sergeant was furious. He ordered all the officers to parade and told them that if the culprits weren't found, our meals would be delayed and our rations would be cut. They were. Either the officers didn't believe his threat or they genuinely couldn't find the thief although they did find two men with bamboo pipes when they conducted the search.

The Nip sergeant left the camp the next day to rejoin his unit. None of us were sorry to see him go although we had to admit that he had done his job well. Discipline amongst the Japs was much stricter and administration had improved while he was with us, but he had lost any popularity he might have earned when he cut our rations.

Ranshaw was caught outside the camp by local civilians. They beat him up and dumped him in a cess pool. The CO had warned us about going outside the camp. Ranshaw had obviously not listened.

Air raids had increased in number. We were having one almost every night. It was great to hear them but we began to long for an undisturbed night's sleep. Night shifts were often halted so that we could go to the shelter. Jerry and I only managed to fill two trucks one night because there had been such a heavy raid that we had spent the greater part of our shift in the air raid shelter. When we got back to the camp, we found that the lads had been in the shelters as well, all except three. For some unknown reason, they had been beaten up by Kaniyasu (a guard) and one of the new guards. The treatment they had meted out had been really rough and we never knew why the three had been picked on. As a result, tension amongst the lads was higher than normal. One night that we didn't have an air raid was the night we received a tobacco ration. That had become unusual. There were very few extras. We hadn't received our pay for weeks on end. Money was short to non existent. The canteen had run out of tea so our cuppas were as short as our smokes.

We were inoculated against typhoid and dysentery, though how any of us could have developed dysentery when our rations had been cut so drastically was beyond my comprehension. Our meal was served up to us in black earthenware bowls and the mixture of rice and beans did little more than cover the bottom of the bowl and it didn't help that the beans were mixed with black grit and stones owing to the warehouse where it had been stored in Tokyo being bombed. Then, when we reported to work, N°2 furnace started giving trouble. It didn't take long for our mood of hope to be replaced by the dark feeling of despondency. The next morning hardly a man could raise his arm high enough to have a drink, let alone get out of bed and go to work. That was how the innoculations had affected us. I had them excused fatigues and managed to borrow a gramophone. It was quite a treat for us all to lie on our beds and listen to the music. The payment of our long overdue wages also helped to lift our spirits. I received my usual 3yen 30 sen, not that there was much on which to spend it. The Nips also made a salt issue. We needed the salt in that climate.

Air raids were continuing with increased frequency. We were also subject to blood tests which we all looked at with apprehension. Our arms still felt stiff from the inoculations and we didn't want any more needles stuck in us. I learned that my blood group was AB which was unusual. Most people were O. We had never heard about blood groups before and it was interesting having them explained to us.

The lads had taken to smoking chrysanthemum leaves. They were so desperate for a cigarette that they would have smoked anything. Fortunately I didn't have the craving as seriously as they did.

Before we went out for our night shift, Paddy Murphy was caught stealing a Dutch lad's chow (food). Silver, another of our men, was accused of stealing the potatoes from the hillside garden. Because of this, we all suffered another cut in our rations. We were now down to less than half rations and we began to suffer for it.

The new Nip sergeant arrived the next morning. He was a big man with a loud voice. He spoke English and had taken to wearing a remodelled R.A.F. cap. He had a grin on his face from ear to ear and we realised that we had a real character. Not that we had time to study him because we were subject to another immediate inoculation. That resulted in yet another lump on my arm.

We were into a period of heavy rain and we wondered if that was deterring the American air raids because we had several nights when there weren't any. Then, when the rain was at its heaviest, we were subject to the biggest raid we had experienced. That was the night N° 3 furnace blew up and, the following day, N° 1 did the same.

We had another of the Jap presentation days that morning and I was given a tin of ginger. Others were given ginger and tea but there was no explanation for this discrimination. Then the C.O. told the officers that there would be a further 75 gram cut in rations. This was because he wanted to build up a reserve of food in case there was an invasion and he was unable to get supplies. They were also told that there would be no transport for anyone other than their own troops. This followed on from Al Silver going walkabout and being picked up at Yama, about $1\frac{1}{2}$ miles from the camp.

Our rations had been cut immediately and I had to report that Freddie Hill and a Dutch lad had lost their Bentos (wooden lunch boxes used for cold food). They had been full at the time so this meant they had gone hungry. There was obviously no honour amongst thieves. We were all hungry. We were all short of food. How then could anyone steal from their own comrades? That was something we couldn't forgive.

My health started to give me concern yet again. I had this weakness in my legs. Walking and moving was an effort and I started taking vitamin B tablets. The doctor told me that I was suffering from malnutrition but there was nothing I could do about that. Thoroughly frustrated and in despair, I resorted to the one thing that could give me comfort, prayer. How much longer, oh Lord, do we have to wait?

The following week, our rations were cut yet again. I wondered how much more our emaciated bodies could take. We were cut from two thirds of our normal ration to one - to 590 grams of mixed rice and beans. The rice was often glutinous, the kind that would have usually been made into rice cakes. Even a tobacco issue couldn't lift my spirits neither could the two new potatoes that we received with our meal that evening, courtesy of the camp's garden, not even when they were accompanied with soy sauce. The morning Tenkos didn't take long fortunately. They were held at 0815 and we were on the job at 0830. One morning we were visited by a dive bomber and we all stopped to watch. That was fascinating until it dropped two bombs and then there was panic!

At the end of July, Captain James woke me to hand out the latest post cards. There was one for me from Joycie telling me about Malcolm's third birthday and another from Catford telling me about the wheelbarrow that my parents had given him. How I wished I could have been with them to see it all. I found it hard to even conjure up a picture in my mind because I had never even seen a photo of him. It was while I was dreaming about home that there was a huge explosion. I immediately thought that it was a delayed action bomb, but investigation showed that the backs of both Nºs 5 and 7 furnaces had broken open. That was another fine mess that we would have to clear up.

We were required to work harder than ever. When we returned from the works, we had to spend time on building the air raid shelters or cleaning up the camp ready for yet another inspection. All the time we were having to combat flies, fleas and mosquitoes. The mozzies had got so bad that mosquito nets were being used as much as possible but they didn't provide much protection.

The meagre rations were taking their toll on the well being of the lads. They had all lost weight and their spirits and morale were low. The persistence of the fleas and mosquitoes didn't help. We kept asking when those Yanks were ever going to come. Food had deteriorated if that was possible. Beans and rice were now in short supply but we were lucky that fish was still available.

Chapter Seven
Was it Peace at last?

August started with a big bang. Another raid was taking place to the west of us and we could see a huge fire about thirty miles away. Fortunately we seemed to be missing the worst of the raids but we weren't missing attacks from the fleas and mozzies. It was impossible to get a good night's sleep because of them. We were all bitten. Mosquito nets were erected over our bed spaces and that helped a bit but if there was the tiniest hole, those mozzies would find it. It was so hot, 96 degrees Fahrenheit in the shade. We were experiencing a heat wave. I went to work in what could only be described as a G string. It wouldn't have gone down well in Bermondsey but it was perfectly acceptable in Kanose. Food had deteriorated even further. There was no soup now and certainly no vegetables. Then the Nips were given peaches at work. There were none for us. I was really peeved about that but I made up for it and went to the canteen and bought five issues of ginger, two of cocoa and two of seaweed. I never thought I would have spent money on such things but I had to have something to improve the diet. To be fair, the cooks were doing the best with what they had but as far as quantity went, they were really short. We had bean mix with herring and almonds for breakfast one day and dried fish with mizu paste and spuds and bean mix for our main meal, about half a bowl. Another day we were served snake with our rice. I would never have thought of eating snake back home but when you're hungry, you don't think of the niceties of life. It tasted like rabbit. There were more bones than flesh to it, but it provided nutritious.

'Wimpey', one of the more cheerful guards, turned up to take Tenko when the C.O. was away one day. He appeared resplendent in long, black boots, armpit high pants and sporting the C.O.'s sword. He announced that the C.O. had ordered that there was to be no more cooking on the nobbies. That didn't worry us. We didn't have anything to cook but some of the lads must have found something because they were caught cooking on them and so nabes were banned from the camp altogether.

When were the Yanks going to come? The air raids continued. One

2 later views of the Kanose Carbide Works

thousand six hundred of their aeroplanes filled the air for almost eleven hours one day. Then, on August 15th, our prayers were answered. Peace, wonderful peace came calling.

August 15th. was immediately declared a rest day. The lads that were already at work returned to their billets even though there had been no official confirmation.

There had been no siren, no warning flag flying at the hill top observation post, no invasion - nothing. All there was, was the C.O. blowing his whistle with all his might, his sword in his hand and bellowing orders for men to stop what they were doing, clean out their shacks and return to

The
clandestine
Carbide
Works light
duties and
'sick' roster

102

camp. During the roll call parade, Ramshaw came wandering back into the camp having been released from eso.

Our friendly Nip Toban was in tears and he told Jimmy Duffy about the surrender, asking him at the same time through his tears what he thought the British and American soldiers would do when they arrived.

There was an air of excitement in the camp but it was tempered with some reserve. We had been fed so many rumours and promises that we didn't dare let this even more wonderful news turn our heads.

There were no more Tenkos. Our own officers took roll call instead. August 16th was a big clear up day. There was a lot of rubbish to get rid of. The Yanks collected all the food they had been saving and shared it out amongst themselves after cooking it over charcoal which they had managed to obtain. It was the first barbecue I had ever seen and it smelt great. I slept outside that night and so did some of the others but most of the lads sat up and just talked quietly.

The C.O. ordered us not to go outside the camp. He was concerned for our safety. He was worried that we would be shot or hurt by the local people who still saw us as enemies. We discussed this and decided to stay in the camp a while longer. The Nip sergeant took a group of us down to the river to swim and collect wood for the cookhouse. Work at the furnaces had resumed but only with Nip labour. The Dutch lads put on a show for us and caused a lot of laughter. It all finished with community singing and everyone sang at the top of their voices. The noise was a sound I will always remember. The lads really gave vent to their feelings of euphoria.

Many of the Japanese granted men (ex-servicemen) left the camp and they were certainly given memorable farewells by our lads, especially Igowa and Spy and their like. There was no attempt for them to make farewell speeches and, in the circumstances, it was just as well. They wouldn't have been appreciated. We were more than pleased to see the back of most of them but there were some who had been helpful. They weren't all bad. We wrote letters for those men saying that they had shown consideration and had not been responsible for any cruelty or unfair treatment. Nishino was one of these.

I spent some time preparing a service for the following Sunday. A lot of Brits attended and so did a few of the Americans. It made all the work I had done worthwhile. Unfortunately I was having trouble with my eyes as well as the weakness in my leg, I knew the diet was the problem but there was nothing I could do about that except wait. Were the Americans ever going to come? We hadn't even been told officially that the war was over.

The C.O. made a hurried visit to Tokyo. When he returned the officers were called to a meeting in the administration building. We were anxious to hear what was happening and our hopes turned to despair when we were told that the war wasn't over. The C.O. spoke to us that evening and said that the war could break out again. We were on the brink of war or peace.

The next day, thirty soldiers and an officer arrived to give us protection. The administration staff were due to leave the next day and they had spent the last few days burning papers. Rumour had it that we would be leaving the camp for a hospital camp. Meanwhile we had to wait. Each man was given half a loaf of bread that evening. That went down very well. When the officers asked about rations, they were told that we were already receiving double that of the local civilians.

Sergeant Dick Whitley, a wireless operator, was our radio wizard who had made a radio from 'spare parts' he had found in his 'workshop' so that we were able to listen in to the news. He was reading a radio manual in camp one day when a guard asked him what he was reading. The guard said he had a radio at home and brought it in for him to be repaired. Jack managed to build up a wireless set with this and other parts he managed to obtain. Some of the essential parts came from the speakers of telephones, which didn't improve Japanese tempers when they failed to work. We hid the finished wireless in the roof space above our beds. The lads were so excited when they heard the news and got to know what was going on in the outside world. We dismantled it and hid the parts when we knew there was to be an inspection but we didn't have time to do that one day when we had a visit from a high ranking Japanese officer. He stood immediatly beneath the radio and delivered a speech. We all silently prayed that he wouldn't twig what was above his head. We didn't have to rely on the rumours. That was how we learned that the Japanese were going to sign the surrender - at long last. The guards' rifles, ammunition and bayonets were to be handed in immediately. We also learned that British troops had landed in Thailand and Singapore and that U.S. forces were due to occupy the capital of Korea. We had waited a long time for this and still we waited. It was the Japanese interpreter that told Doctor Robinson about the atomic bomb. I think a lot of our men would not have survived another winter in captivity if those two bomb had not been dropped. They had had enough.

I started feeling really unwell and suffered nose bleeds. When the C.O. asked for volunteers to write P.O.W. on the roofs of the buildings, I chickened out. My aching legs would not have made it. The Nips were sure that the Yanks would be flying over us any day and dropping food supplies. We'd been without washing water and electricity in the camp now for thirty days. In some ways, the conditions in these waiting days were the worst we had experienced.

An area was cleared where football matches could be played and quiz contests were organised. Those tests of general knowledge showed how much one could forget. Ted Pedder thought an octogenarian was an animal of the Stone Age. Another lad thought a hypotenuse was a kipper. Ten days had passed since the 'Armistice' and there was no news and no sign from the allies that they knew of our existence. A U.S. aeroplane did fly over and drop supplies but not to us. We were in the hills so were not on any flight path. We were told that the drops had only been made over the flat ground. That wasn't any use to us but at least we knew food was coming. We waited.

Bales of clothes were brought into the camp and I was issued with Red Cross boots that fitted me a treat. I now had three pairs of boots and two pairs of rubber shoes. If only they had been available when I had been working and had had to exist with sandals I had made from rubber tyres. I was also issued with wide bottomed trousers, white undershirts and pants. We were beginning to feel like our old selves and much more human.

At the end of the month, the electricity came back on and we were told that we would be moving within a month. But the C.O. told our officers that the terms of the Armistice had still not been signed.

Fl. Lt. Chater asked the C.O. for another bulb for his billet and the Jap reached up, took his own bulb out and gave it to him. It was a complete turnaround. It started to become bewildering, but not so bewildering that we didn't appreciate the change. The feel of clean clothes was wonderful as was the feeling of hope for the future. We knew this was now within our reach. The C.O. asked our officers to enquire if any of the men wished to stay in Japan. I'll draw a veil over their response!

It was the following Monday that rumours really started to run amok when an official was closeted with the C.O. in the administration block and the staff started getting drunk. Our officers were invited across for a drink. The lads were convinced that we would be leaving by the 30th. They were even more convinced when Wimpey came into the hut shouting, 'All dance and music'.

But nothing else happened. We were issued with more clothes and black shiny bowls for our food but there was no extra food to put in them. It seemed that we were the only camp not to receive food supplies. The Nip interpreter disappeared to Tokyo to find out why and the Nip sergeant headed off to Niigata to try and get flour and meat supplies. Our meals were now plain rice and weak soup with the occasional cucumber or green tomato. The C.O. promised that he would have a goat and pig killed for our last meal and, that as soon as the Armistice was signed, the camp would be handed over to us officially. He also said that if we had any complaint to make against the granted men, we must lay the blame on him and not the Nipponese concerned.

Then a B 29 flew over and we rushed out to watch and that was all it did, - flew over. The next camp to us, some thirty miles away, was receiving regular food supplies that were being dropped by parachute. Using our bed sheets we set out P.O.W. in large letters on the ground but still the B 29s failed to notice us. Captain Hewitt wrote a letter to the Commander of the U.S. Contact Forces.

We were receiving news bulletins regularly now. We were told of the Japanese surrender and the Emperor's command that all Japanese were to cease fighting. We also understood that some of his men had refused to obey this order. It was all going on in the big world out there. Meanwhile, we were feeling forgotten. It was obvious that we were not going to leave the camp on August 30th.

The temperature suddenly dropped and we knew that the typhoon season was approaching. It was also Queen Wilhelmina's 65th birthday. The Dutch put on a show to celebrate and the Dutch know how to put on a show. It started with both our national anthems and we sung them with gusto. And so we left August behind, in many ways the most disconcerting month of all. At the end of it we were left waiting, waiting, waiting.

September 1st and Captain Hewitt received the answer to his letter. He said that he would pass all messages on and asked us to be patient for a few more days. He was sure that food would reach us soon. Meanwhile they were trying to get prisoners to the ships as soon as possible. That letter brought loud cheers from everyone. The Nip sergeant brought the letter and also 1,500 cigarettes to be distributed. Then we were told that from the next day, we would each be receiving a kilogram of rice each. We finished the day with a sing song. We were confident that freedom was imminent.

The rail box car arrived outside the barracks at 0730 hours. We believed that our relief supplies had arrived from Niigata. And what did it contain, - gum - gum and matches - more gum and more matches - more..... by the boxload. Someone had been at the supplies before we got them.

I managed to get a copy of Time magazine. I read it out to the lads. It was out of date but it told us of the battles that had been going on and what had been happening in a world that had been hidden from us.

As soon as we knew the surrender had been signed, a lot of men got out

*Just some of the postcards given as 'Farewell' gifts by
Japanese guards at Kanose Carbide Camp after the
surrender*

of the camp and wandered round the works. We had plenty of clothing now and we handed bundles of it through the windows to the Nips who had been working with us on the furnaces. They were given so much that they couldn't carry it all away. Some of the lads made it to the village and were invited into homes to drink sake. They were absolutely drunk when they returned to camp.

I was still helping to make our flag, from my own P.O.W. numbered (142) white bed sheet, coloured with red and blue crayon. We took the rope from a kit bag. A lot of lads who had been helping were getting involved in other things. We were feeling a lot better for the extra rice but we were still waiting for our food drop. We saw B 29s flying overhead and making drops at Niigata but not to us. We carried on waiting. We weren't as worried about lack of supplies, our rice rations were far more than we needed but it would have been nice if there had been some sign that the outside world knew we existed.

Then Captain Hewitt was told that he had to go to Niigata to meet the Governor of Minnesota. When he returned, he told us that we would be leaving the camp in four days time. His news was greeted with three hearty cheers. Three days later, on September 5th, half a truck load of supplies arrived, that afternoon another full truckload turned up. They couldn't get rid of the supplies quickly enough and we wouldn't have time to make the most of them if we really were leaving at 0700 hours the next morning.

Jerry Murray and I took a walk down to the village. It was wonderful to be able to take a walk again after all those years of internment. We found a bamboo pole in a garden which was ideal as a flagpole for our flag. A frightened Japanese woman let us have it for a supply of matches and gum. The villagers seemed to have become as fond of gum as the Yanks. I also swopped a pair of R.A.F. trousers and tunic for an old pipe which I wanted to take home as a souvenir. Nips were wandering in and out of the camp all day asking for supplies and we were pleased to supply them. All the villagers including tiny tots were asking for gum. We had plenty to eat and a good variety. We had never been so full or suffered from so much flatulence.

There was so much excitement and sake. Fl. Lt. Chater asked the N.C.O.s to have a drink with him and it appeared the doctor had been supplying the men with neat alcohol and things really got out of hand until sleep set in.

September 6th dawned

'THE GREAT DAY' - WE WERE GOING 'HOME'.

Chapter Eight
Homeward Journey

The first station party was roused at 0400 hours and the second at 0430. Nobody wanted any rice. The flags were unfurled. The Yanks went first with their stars and stripes made from parachute silk held high. Food for the journey had already been taken down to the station, enough to last a week let alone a day. The Nip C.O. made a final speech of farewell and shook everyone by the hand. The groups lined up behind their hand made flags and we were off, marching through the gates for the very last time. Villagers lined the road and scrambled for packets of gum that we threw to them as we passed. There was plenty of room on the train. Sergeant Dick Whitley and I had a compartment to ourselves. We fixed the flag outside the compartment to wave us along the way. The food that was distributed to us on the journey was five times more than we needed. We were given ham and eggs, chicken soup, biscuits, butter, cheese, fudge, chocolate, toffee, coffee, milk, fruit and bacon. We threw lots of it out to the people on the stations we passed. We couldn't eat that much after all those years of near starvation. In any case, we were already full.

All the same, I spent some silent moments looking out of the window, wondering at the beauty of the scenery through which we were travelling and thinking of my beloved family and silently thanking God for starting me on this journey back to them.

We saw our first military soldiers on Tokyo Station. It was wonderful to shake hands with them. They gave us a great reception. Our Union Jack (3) remained waving proudly from the back of the train until we reached Yokohama at 0945 hours. That was where we saw our first American girls, our first non Japanese women for more than three years. They were walking up and down the platform offering chocolates, candies and cigarettes and pretty good back chat as well. U.S. soldiers restrained the crowds of Japanese sightseers that thronged the platform. Lorries were lined up outside to take us to our next destination. When the engines started up, it was like music to our ears.

(3) See page 132

109

We were directed down to the docks where, after a bowl of soup and a wonderful mug of coffee, we had a medical inspection and went through a processing shower spray. When the inspection was completed, we were ushered to camp beds in a huge terminal building and told to be ready the next morning at 0700 hours when we would be flown out to Okinawa and Manila. There was no doubt about it, the Yanks were well organised.

Before I left on the plane next morning, I managed to send a telegram to Joyce saying *'Freed by the Americans'*.

It was the shortest message I ever sent anyone.

We had breakfast before we left, fried chips and sausages, not once, not twice but three times plus the mugs of coffee. We left by train for the airfield at Atsugi and I think we were all silenced by the sight that met our eyes. There were more aeroplanes lined up than I had ever seen taxis lined up outside one of the main railway stations in London. They were mainly C54 cargo carriers and they shone in the morning light. First of all, we were introduced to the canteen facilities and boy, did we make the most of them. I fed until I could take no more. We handed over our bags for storage in the nose of the aircraft and climbed into the plane and strapped ourselves in. The flight lasted from 1630 hours until 2200 hours. Our last sight of Japan was of a glorious sunset and Mount Fujiyama before we turned our attention to the south and saw the next lights on Long Rope Island, Okinawa. We were kept waiting on the Tarmac for an hour until a lorry arrived to take us to Beach Camp. We had doughnuts, ice cream and coffee. We were issued with blankets and mess kit and shown to our tents where, surprise, surprise, I met up with my old pal Les Fulluck as well as some of the others. And that wasn't all. We were greeted by a military band. What a wonderful touch that was. Some of the lads were in tears. I finally hit the sack at 0130 hours on Saturday morning. But I was up at dawn and heading off for breakfast, scrumptious scrambled eggs, new bread, butter, jam and coffee with milk and sugar - twice. I don't think I had ever enjoyed a breakfast so much.

As the day warmed up, it was time for tiffin, sausages, bread and cheese, iced coffee, ice cream - twice. Some of the lads managed more but there was still dinner to come in the evening. We certainly made up for all those tasteless meals we had endured in captivity.

During the evening, names were announced over the loud speakers of men who were scheduled to move on the next day. My name was called out to be ready to move off at 0400 hours on Monday, September 10th.

I had been trying to reduce the size of my kit but I really did not know what else to throw out and it didn't help when we were issued with American uniforms as well.

I needed no encouragement to rise the next morning. I was up by 0200 hours, eager and ready to take this next step towards home. We were loaded into a B24 bomber without any sign of the scrumptious breakfast we had expected but it was just as well because bad weather was forecast. In fact, the flight took an hour longer than expected. We flew between Formosa and the Chinese coast and landed at Manila at 0200 hours on Tuesday, September 11th. A band welcomed us at the canteen and made us feel like real V.I.P.s. Very sadly one of the planes flew into the storm and was lost into the sea. One of those on board had been Corporal Botting, the lad who had machined the tabs and insignia onto our flag - what a tragedy.

We had cakes and coffee before being moved on to our camp. I was assigned to tent 20E which I shared with seven of the Royal Scots Regiment from Hong Kong, some of the same lads that had had been among the unfortunates on the SS Lisbon Maru. The change of company was as good as a tonic. It helped to listen to their stories. We had had a grim time but theirs had been grimmer.

We were given a medical examination and I weighed in at ten stone, nine pounds - wow! We were given sheets for our beds and received Red Cross comfort bags which contained a towel, toothpaste, talcum powder, a razor, shoe polish and pyjamas. It was just as well that I'd turfed out some of my kit before the flight.

We experienced showery weather and lots of mud while we waited for our ship home. The nights were hot and humid. We spent our time catching up on film shows but even those began to pall. We were anxious to make that next step towards home. Some of the lucky R.A.F. ex P.O.W.s were flown home but my name wasn't called out. Fortunately the canteen was open all day and there were frequent issues of cigarettes, candies and cookies. We made the most of the largesse. The days bordered on being boring despite the fact that we were all relishing the feeling of freedom. There was a piano and radio in the canteen so that gave us a change from the continually running films.

My name was called on Sunday, September 23rd. I was to be drafted on the 'Admiral Hughes', a US liberty ship, the following day. I had to sort out my kit yet again and answer letters that I had received from my Joycie and my sister Lily. I also wrote to my mother-in-law, 'Dickie'.

Monday, September 24th, we were checked over, fed our midday meal and ready to go. Sergeant Sid Ward and myself found a cool spot by the canteen doors and waited until our numbers were called. I had to force down this feeling of excitement. I was about to go on the next step of my journey back to my loved ones. My number was 536 and, at last, I was called out to the lorry. It was a fifteen mile trip to the docks from the airfield. All the buildings that we passed showed signs of devastation and the dockside warehouses had been demolished by the Japanese before they left. At one point we saw an invasion barge on the road manned by British naval personnel. It was flying the White Ensign. That brought a lump to my   throat.

We boarded the Admiral Hughes, a U.S. liberty ship, immediately. As I struggled up the gangway with my kit, I was handed a packet of Lucky Strike cigarettes and a packet of gum. I don't think the Americans would have survived the war without their gum.

Almost as soon as we were on board, the announcement came over the tannoy, "All ashore who are going ashore". We set sail at 1700 hours.

I was in compartment 74 on the third deck down. Going down almost vertical ladders with all my kit was incredibly difficult but I made it. It was stiflingly hot and my clothes were soon wet with perspiration. I wasted no time finding the showers. Fortunately ice cold water was available at all times from numerous faucets round the ship. There were 4,000 personnel on board and everything seemed to be accomplished in double quick time, even our meals. These were served on a tray system and the troops stood at tables to eat them. It didn't worry us where, what or how we ate them, after being without for so long. We were fed good, tasty nutritious meals.

We could still see the Philippines, 24 hours out from Manilla. During the early part of our voyage, we passed a small fort which had been taken by the Nips and then fortified. They battered any ship approaching Manilla from there. It was so strongly fortified that there was no way it could be taken or destroyed by bombing, so night patrol vessels dashed up to it, pumped it full of gasoline and set it alight. No-one would venture near it for a long time because of the foul smell of the burned Nips.

We also saw Corregidor opposite Bataan. It was here that the Yanks who had been with us in our camp had fought and been captured.

Generally the days were warm and sunny and we lazed on the decks Film shows took place regularly on a large screen that had been set up on

One of the special public relation touches shown by our Canadian hosts. It made us all feel that bit more special and, after our treatment as P.O.W.s, helped to minimise the humiliation we had experienced

An aerial view of the business section of Vancouver BC

Canadian Pacific Railway Co's Docks in Vancouver BC

Postcards we were given by the Canadian Red Cross Society. They never did fail us.

On the way home, via Canadian National Railway, 18th October, 1945. During the trip I wrote a postcard to Joycie and enjoyed Red Cross hospitality all the way.

the deck. Compared with our previous voyage from Java, this one was sheer luxury. It was like being on a no expense spared luxury cruise and I appreciated every minute of it.

We crossed the International Date Line on October 2nd, 1945. That gave us our second Tuesday in one week. We were 2,500 nautical miles from San Fransisco. Then we were told that our destination had changed and we were making for Seattle. As long as we were heading east, they could make for wherever they liked as far as I was concerned. The weather had grown cooler but it was still uncomfortably hot below decks. My bunk was the top one and it was really near the deck head. I knew that only too well when I sat up without thinking. I could put up with any amount of discomfort. Every mile, every hour was bringing me nearer home.

Then our expected date of arrival was delayed. One boiler had burst and had to be repaired which slowed us down. Then the other boiler was out of action and we were only using one screw. Our destination was changed yet again to Vancouver in Canada.

I was still having trouble with my legs that had started in Kanose. My legs and feet were swollen and I couldn't stand for too long. Even sitting with my legs dangling caused them to swell and ache. To add to this I had a heat rash all over my arms and back and a problem with pimples. Other than that my physical condition had improved considerably. I was two stone heavier than I had been at Kanose and I had muscles now where I had only been skin and bones. Clambering up and down the ladders from deck to deck helped to tone my muscles.

There were no complaints about the catering. The variety and quantity was incredible to our eyes. There were over 50,000 books in the library, so many that I was bewildered when I first went to choose a book. I had become used to the few that had been available in the camp. Ball games were something else. These were broadcast non stop for the sake of the crew and we couldn't understand what they were talking about. We had no idea of the games the Americans supported. The worst thing was the volume of the broadcasts. Loudspeakers were everywhere. There was nowhere you could escape from the racket. If it wasn't games, it was hot music and that was just as bad.

Sunday services were held on the upper deck. The weather was getting colder as we travelled further north and we were advised to wear winter clothing. British personnel were to leave the ship at Victoria Dock, four miles short of the island. We started sorting out our things straight away, ready to disembark.

Tuesday, October 9th dawned as a misty, chilly morning. The outline of the coast seen through the mist was sheer magic. It was wonderful. We were coming nearer home. By noon, we had sighted the outline of Vancouver Island and then we were drawing into the dock and we were receiving the greatest welcome that anyone could ever experience. As we entered the harbour, all the ships there were blowing their sirens and the church bells were ringing. As our ship drew in alongside, an army band and a naval one were playing. The folks of Esquinalt gave us an even greater welcome than the one we had received from the folks of Durban all those years ago. Only service personnel and relations of men on board had been allowed on the quayside. As we drew alongside, the Canadians were throwing up apples to us and we were throwing back Japanese coins and notes. They were no use to us any more.

Army, navy and airforce personnel were separated on disembarking. We were to go to Pat Bay, 17 miles away but we had to undergo a medical examination before we could go there. I sent a cable to Joyce as soon as I had the opportunity and also posted the letters I had written on board. Then Sid Ward and I went for a walk. We met up with some soldiers from the Canadian army who had fought in Europe. They took us to a bar where we had turkey sandwiches and beer, returning to our billet at 0030 hours. What a day that had been.

Our beds had springs and crisp white sheets and soft pillows, absolute luxury. There were no bed boards, no bunks. We had proper beds. Did we sleep that night! I woke up just in time to have breakfast before joining the transport for Pat Camp and what a day that turned out to be. We collected our kit when we arrived and had a quick look round when we were invited to join the WAAFs in their lounge. They really looked after us. Then we had to go to the tailors to be fitted with trousers and jackets. All our meals were taken in the sergeants' mess where, besides plentiful supplies of food, there was beer, beer and yet more beer. The merriment continued all day finishing with a dance and a party. I had an excellent partner and spent some time with her and her fiancee. They promised to come and visit us when they visited England. I went to bed at 0130 the following morning. The next day was similar. We had an absolutely wonderful time but it was more than that. We were with our own people. They had fought with us. They spoke the same language as we did and many of them had relations back in England. I don't think I could have kept up the social life much longer. I was a little relieved when we were told that we would be leaving at 0730 hours the following morning and that we were to wear our proper uniforms. The Canadians had given us a wonderful time, but we were ready to move on. We wanted to get home.

We travelled across Canada by Canadian National Railway and we were greeted and applauded at every stop we made. We saw the magnificence of the Rockies and travelled through the country from west to east until we reached Halifax in Nova Scotia. There we embarked on the Ile de France and set sail almost immediately for England and Home. I can't explain our feelings when we saw the English coast for the first time. All I know is that a silence descended over us all. We were all wrapped up with our own thoughts. Some were crying. My thoughts were with Joyce and the thought of seeing my son Malcolm for the first time. I longed to know what he looked like.

My plans were for the future. I was determined to put the past behind me.

We had to wait outside the docks until the morning at Southampton. We all felt let down at not being able to dock straight away. The next morning we went by train to Cosford and our first contact with officialdom. There was none of the enthusiastic welcome we had received in Canada. Now we were treated with 100 per cent efficiency by the RAF. There were medical examinations, fed and watered and then sleep. The following morning, after breakfast, we were given full details of our journeys home, times of trains, passes and English money to see us through. We had almost forgotten its value.

I shared my taxi at Chatham with two others and was soon on my way to Heather Cottage and there was my Joycie. We fell into each others arms. We didn't need to speak. We were together again and that was all that mattered. Then we went upstairs. I was going to see my son and I suddenly found myself shaking. I had waited so long for this moment.

He was asleep in his cot, looking so innocent. Joyce lifted him up and he stirred. "Malcolm," she said, "this is your Daddy."

Malcolm mumbled a reply and fell asleep again. I kissed him and we put him back in his cot. Until that moment his Daddy had been a photo on the wall.

I had to return to Cosford and on to R.A.F. Hednesford where I was fitted with my demob suit. It was a shock to hear the tailor say that I needed a portly fitting. Joyce had expected an emaciated figure when I returned home. I had weighed 8 stone when I left Japan. U.S. hospitality had changed that. I must have looked more like a Michelin man at 13 stone 2lbs but it all sorted out when I started work.

*Our mothers enjoying a
quiet tete-a-tete in the
gardens of my sister Elsie
at Bessells Green,
Sevenoaks, Kent in 1965.
My mother (left) was
living with my sister and
her husband Stanley
Farmer, at the time*

*Joyce, myself and friends at the
Town Hall, Chatham, for a Round
Table 41, Anniversary Dinner/
Dance in 1950.*

*At a P.O.W. Reunion, run by the
Red Cross, in 1996, at West
Studdal Farm, near Dover. I am
arrowed.*

118

Dysentery figures mounted as the voyage proceeded and
when we reached Japan we had about three hundred cases, about
one third of them serious.

On arrival at Simoniseki, Japan I was ordered ashore
with my party.   I asked permission for some of the sick to
be left aboard for hospital treatment.   Five were allowed
to remain aboard.   On shore I asked the new interpreter to
request the officer waiting to receive us if one or two others
could be put back on to the ship.   Four more were re-
embarked.   Some of the men had discarded their fouled
clothes, and were wrapped in their blankets.   The weather
was bitter (28th Nov).   Some of the men had sole-less boots
and wrapped their feet with scraps of cloth.

We were taken to a camp in the Japanese Alps, (Mitsushima). The journey took 30 hours in a train and one man
died en route.   We were quartered in flimsy huts with gaps
between the boarding. We were all in tropical kit.   The
temperature was about 22 deg. Fahrt.   Captured British
battle dress was issued to us on the night of our arrival.

Details of this camp ought to be in Air Ministry hands
already, since the second senior Officer Prisoner, S/Ldr
Blanchard has given evidence in Yokohama last month at the
trial of the Japanese Camp Commandant and other Mitsushima
personnel.   Here is a brief resume, however.

The camp was composed of 189 R.A.F.and Army personnel,
including 14 Officers and 3 Officers and 79 American other
ranks.   One Dutch-Javanese M.O.

I was there as Senior Officer R.A.D. prisoner for
about 8 months.   During that time 50 prisoners died including 5 R.A.F.Officers.   Deaths occurred from dysentery, pneumonia,
diphtheria and other causes and were all accelerated by malnut-
tition, cold, lack of medical supplies and neglect generally.

Greatcoats and underwear were not issued untill late in
January. Heating was allowed after for about one hour a day
from the end of January until early in March. This privilege
was often rescinded wantonly by the Japanese duty N.C.O. Food
was coarse and often uncooked owing to, the Japanese dragging
the fire from under the boilers in order to warm themselves.
Sick men were ordered to work and usually beaten up if they repot
ted sick. I was frequently assaulted for trying to have sick men
kept off the working parade. One Red Cross box was issued while
I was in the camp. Bulk Red Cross cocoa, sugar and fruits were
stolen by the Japanese. There was one visit from a Red Cross
Representative, and Cory, the senior American Officer and myself
were eaten up and kicked for telling him about conditions in
the Camp. I sent Mr C.P.Robertson the cutting from the Times
which reported this incident.

The Japanese C.O. left the running of the Camp to his
N.C.O.s and ignored all my verbal and written requests for
better food, medical teatment and betterment of working and
other conditions in general.

near Buitenzorg. Wing Commander Matthews was senior Officer *but* prisoner here for most of the time, and as he has doubtless *previously* made his report on the situation there I shall not duplic- *mentioned* ate it. I would like to say, however, that apart from a certain amount of mild slapping, conditions were not unduly hard.

Some time in October 1942, (18th), I was detailed to take 500 men to Japan. These were mostly R.A.F. personnel, including a number of Chinese and other natives from the Special Technical Corps formed in Singapore. There were 19 officers apart from myself, including two Light Anti-Aircraft officers and two half-caste Javanese-Dutch Medical Officers .

We were taken ashore at Singapore and marched through the town and after a few days at Changi re- embarked for Japan. The two L.A.A.C. officers and other one sick R.A.F.officer were left behind and my party was reduced to 200. We sailed on the 30th October for Japan. The ship was greatly overcrowded. About 1200 mixed British, Dutch, Australian and American_s were quartered in the forepart of the ship. The rest of the ship was occupied by Japanese. Lavatory accommodations was grossly inadequate and the water supply was meagre and was largely wasted by the Japanese who used our fresh water to wash themselves and their clothes.

Dysentery broke out within a week of leaving. My party was the only one with any medical supplies which naturally we shared with the rest of the prisoners on board. Major Andrews and myself nade repeated efforts to have the seriously ill personnel put ashore at the first opportunity, (Saigon), and to obtain drugs for the sick. We were unsuccessful and the Japanese interpreter usually lost his temper with us and pushed us out of the cabin.

Dysentery fatalities started after leaving Saigon. We buried between 35 and 40 at sea. We tried again to have sick put ashore at Formosa where we arrived on the 16th November. This was agin refused. The ship was now in the most insanitry condition. There were only five latrines for twelve hundred men. The latrine queue was usually an average of 25 for 24 hours a day. Dysentery patients squatted over the rails. At our request one of the least bad Japanese provided,in the improvised sick quarters. tubs for those who were too weak to get up to the deck. 40 stools a day was not uncommon in this type of dysentery. The situation was aggravated by weather. During heavy rolling one patient and bucket fell from the tween decks to the hold and died shortly afterwards. Seasickness was rife amongst the chinese.

Report by ex-Squadron Leader David Grant obtained from the Public Records Office, Kew

Chapter Nine
Return to Mitsushima & Reconciliation

The most important thing was to spend time with my wife and son and to visit my family. Then my cousin, Ernest Salt, who was now a director of my old company, phoned up and suggested I called in to meet the Company Chairman. After a general tour, he asked me if I wanted my old job back and I was pleased to have it. Jobs for ex-servicemen weren't that easy. I was entitled to 103 days release leave but I went back to work as soon as I could. My back pay minus tax and Joyce's stopped allowances didn't go far so I wanted to get on with my life, to return to normality. Wanting to forget Japan and the privations I had experienced wasn't easy. My boss told everyone where I had been. I didn't like it at first and then it didn't worry me any more. I was happy to be home.

The job proved fascinating. I was a salesman attached to branches in Rochester, Maidstone and Tonbridge. There were no company cars then and I had to go everywhere by public transport. Roberts Adlard were roofing contractors and builders merchants. There was a great shortage of building materials in those post war days and a lot of our supplies were imported. It was a fascinating job. Central heating came in. Then I found myself going to France for a course on floor tiling. There was never a dull moment. I was promoted

Graham and Takako's visit to the dam was reported in the local Teuryu-Mura District newspaper

8 Ford Close,
Bridge, Canterbury,
Kent. CT4 5LX England.

Telephone +44(0)1227830560

A Message To The Community Of The Village Of Mitsushima.

My son GRAHAM comes to you with a message of goodwill from one who was in this area which was known as Tokyo No.3. during the war years of 1942-1945 as a prisoner of war.

Memories of those days have mellowed although they are still retained after over 50 years. Re-reading my diaries, which were written during that time, I can still relive the atmosphere and anxiety of the time but now on reflection I can appreciate my good fortune in surviving the experiences.
I hope to publish the details of my diaries and in doing so hope to bring a moderate approach to my period of capture to somewhat counter the many recorded atrocities by members of the DAI NIPPON GUN. It is true to say that in times of war these distressing happenings always take place but also there are the opposite and fair considerate situations which get overlooked.

My son and his wife TAKAKO and also other members of my family have shown a strong desire to look further into this period of my life and therefore have been anxious to make contact with your present community.

I send you my best wishes for happiness and understanding of international goodwill on behalf of all others like-minded POW's who were at MITSUSHIMA camp.

Sincerely,

Ex. Sgt.. W.C.Rose R.A.F.V.R. 917922
24th March 1998

My message taken by Graham and Takako to Mitsushima - May 1997

122

within the firm and eventually moved to Canterbury to open a new branch. That meant we had to leave Heather Cottage. We moved to Bridge where we have found friendship and happiness. Our Christian faith and love for each other have seen us through any difficulty we have encountered and that is how I have tried to look at my incarceration in Japan.

When I came home, I was determined to shut the P.O.W. period completely out of my mind but that hasn't always been possible. Sometimes a simple thing may bring back memories I thought I had long forgotten and, without warning experienced a sudden feeling of depression reminiscent of my feelings back at Mitsushima and Kanose. It happened and I have had to accept that it happened. It was a very testing time. I have never sought out other people who shared my experiences in the camps. and have never joined any society that has tried to keep those memories alive. Having to face up to what happened on my own was hard but it has been my wife and my family that has given me the strength to do so.

The years have slipped by, Joyce and I have been married for 64 years and we have experienced many good times. We have had our ups and downs but the most difficult time was the war time separation, almost five years in all. Being a POW was a very testing time but I got through it with prayer and a resolve to overcome. I have often been asked what I thought of the Japanese people. My reply was always that not all of the Japanese people were responsible for the atrocities. I am only too grateful that I was given the strength, mentally and physically, to survive. As a consequence, I have been able to forgive, if not completely forget, those unfortunate years.

One of our happiest experiences has been to welcome our Japanese daughter in law, Takako, into the family. I would never have though such a thing would have brought us so much happiness. I had felt surprise when my middle son Graham brought her home to meet us. This was the first Japanese person I had met since the war. I told her I had been to Japan and she said she hoped I had had a good time. No! I had not had a good time! Graham explained why I had been in Japan. Takako had not known the details of the POW camps in Japan. Now she was going home and she said that she would find the camp where I had worked. She did, but it took her three years. Mitsushima is such a small dot on the map that she couldn't find where it was. By chance whilst in a library she stumbled upon a dam which had been built during the war and that was how she discovered it. Takako went up to see the site where the camp had been and called at the council offices to ask directions. The manager was really interested in why she wanted to know and arranged for a car to take her to the dam. Graham and Takako were married in 1994. Three years later, they both went to Mitsushima and they took a letter of reconciliation from me.

I am a Christian. It was time for me to forgive even if I could never forget. All the same, I hesitated when I was invited to return to Japan in 1999. The visit was made possible by Keiko Holmes of AGAPE, an organisation which is based on reconciliation. The trip was financed by the Japanese themselves.

All the same I set off with a feeling of doubt and trepidation.

My son, Malcolm, flew out from Australia and joined me in Tokyo. We received friendliness and interest and first class treatment everywhere we went. The New Otani Hotel we stayed in at Tokyo, was the most luxurious hotel I had ever seen. There were 24 of us ex Far East prisoners of war and realised I wasn't the only one that had doubts. Through the offices of AGAPE, arrangements had been made for me to visit Mitsushima.

We went first class by bullet train for the initial part of the journey, accompanied by an interpreter Keiko McNichol and an NHK reporter, stopping overnight at a hotel and then going on to Hiroaka, the village beside Mitsushima dam by local train.

How can I explain my feelings as the train sped through the countryside along the same route that I had taken 60 years earlier. However much I tried to banish these thoughts from my mind, they returned with a vividness and pain that made it difficult to breathe. In reality, I was travelling through modern Japan but my thoughts were of the same journey earlier, cold, hungry and dejected. As we drew nearer our destination, those thoughts became stronger and more painful. The screech of the brakes as we climbed the slopes was the same screech we had heard all those years ago. The carriages tilted just as I had remembered they tilted before.

We had been travelling through a long series of tunnels and then we emerged into the bright sunlight and there was the lake and the river and the dam and the back cloth of mountains and we were drawing in to the station.

It had been bitterly cold in 1942. Now we stepped out from an air conditioned train into a temperature of 90 degrees Fahrenheit. I was wearing my very English three piece suit and trilby hat when the heat hit me like a brick wall. There facing us on the platform was a sea of faces and that was the start of one of the most memorable days of my life. We had expected to have a quiet walk round the village and the site of our old camp and suddenly we were faced with a sea of smiling applauding people. Barriers were in place to keep them back. Facing us was a group of smartly dressed dignitaries and beside them were the press and television crews. Before I had time to catch my breath a 'hedgehog' was thrust in front of my face and I was asked to give my feelings at returning to my place of captivity. I was forced to deflect this question in order to keep my emotions under control I felt stunned and astonished by the reception. I felt that Malcolm beside me was equally bemused.

We were escorted to a big, black sedan and driven to the dam, followed by a long line of cars carrying photographers. We were invited to visit the museum and walk across the dam. After taking a few photographs, the photographers disappeared and, surprise, surprise, there they were waiting for us when we got to the other side. So we had another photograph session. Then we went to the school. This is where the camp had been. If there was any emotion left it would have been here. But this was where all the hurt and tension faded away. This is where I finally came to terms with my time as a prisoner of war. I thought I had forgotten them but I realised then, I had merely hidden them. These children were the grandchildren, in some cases the great grandchildren, of those who had been our captors. They knew nothing of the war. They, like everyone else I met, were offering friendship. They wanted to know everything. Where had I slept? What was in the Red Cross parcel? And I found I could answer without any feeling of hurt or hatred. Those feelings had been banished and I now started to relax and start enjoying the visit.

We didn't have time to linger. We went to a reception given by the Mayor and local dignitaries and had a lunch. It was a good job we had a translator with us because nobody spoke English, but Keiko McNichol was really skilful.

Then we were told we would be given a short rest but no sooner had we settled down and started to catch our breath then Keiko McNichol ushered two elderly ladies in. They had lived in the village when we had been POWs and they chattered away talking about those days. Then we were ushered into yet another building. A banner was stretched across the lane and it said "Welcome back, William Rose". We were shown into a lift, the doors of which shut sharply behind us leaving the dignitaries on the floor. When the lift doors opened again, there they were waiting to greet us.

They must have run up the stairs.

We were escorted into a hall where people were sitting round tables. The applause exploded as we entered. There were speeches, which Keiko translated. I made a speech, so did my son Malcolm. Whilst head boy gave a welcoming speech in English we noticed there was a couple at one table who had not taken their eyes from us. They were Nishino's son and daughter. He had been the one armed guard who had tried to help us. It was good to meet them later. They brought us gifts from their mother, some embroidered decorative balls and home-made scent. We were entertained by dancers and music. Then food was served but little time to eat it. We were whisked off again. This time driven through the mountains. It was dark when we arrived at our next venue and given just ten minutes to tidy up for our official reception. This was Japanese style and was given by local businessmen. The tables and seats were at floor level, and the food was heated by little stoves on the tables. We watched what our hosts were doing and copied them. There were more speeches. We were so thankful that Keiko McNichol had travelled with us because amongst others we had a visitor from Kanose who couldn't speak English. Keiko had to leave us at 8.45pm which left me struggling with my wartime Japanese and gestures until about 10pm. Eventually it was time for bed. At last I shed my three piece suit and donned Japanese style pyjamas but there was no chance to sleep. Keiko knocked on our door and asked if the reporter could ask us some more questions. They stayed for four hours.

Neither of us slept. We felt as though we had been on a roller coaster and needed time to unwind. We got up at 4 o'clock to go for a quiet walk, but we had not gone more than a hundred metres when we were surrounded by a group of friendly people. Breakfast was ready, would we please go with them? So, at half past four in the morning we sat down to a sumptuous breakfast,: rice, smoked fish, and cold fried eggs.

I rejoined the rest of the group in Tokyo and Malcolm flew home. We visited Hiroshima and Osaka. We went to museums and other camp sites and churches. And always there was this feeling of friendliness and interest, always there was this wish to make up for anything that had happened in the past. It was time for reconciliation. We all felt more at peace with ourselves and the past as we returned home.

My sons again have contacted Nishino's children and I continue to receive letters and cards from the children at the school and my other new Japanese friends.

One boy wrote, "I still remember the warmth of your hand when I shook hands with you."

My life had now turned full circle.

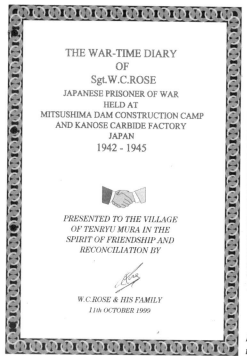

THE WAR-TIME DIARY
OF
Sgt. W.C. ROSE
JAPANESE PRISONER OF WAR
HELD AT
MITSUSHIMA DAM CONSTRUCTION CAMP
AND KANOSE CARBIDE FACTORY
JAPAN
1942 - 1945

PRESENTED TO THE VILLAGE
OF TENRYU MURA IN THE
SPIRIT OF FRIENDSHIP AND
RECONCILIATION BY

W.C. ROSE & HIS FAMILY
11th OCTOBER 1999

The first letter from home

Front page of the diary copy presented
to the people of Haraoka

The Dam

Views of the visit to Mitsushima

Nishino's family on the centre table

Message to Mr. william Rose

Welcome to Tennryu Village, Mr. William Rose.
You have got over your bitter memories of the very hard time here at Mitushima,
at your precious and valuable age, caused by that disgusting war.

All the villagers including The Mayor Mr. Hata would like to give you a warm
welcome with the deepest respect.

Thank you very much for the last year's visiting to our school of your second
son Mr. Graham Rose and his wife Mrs. Takako Rose. At that time they brought us
your message. It said that it was true that distressing happenings always took
place in those days, but also there were the opposite and fair considerate
situations which got overlooked. We were impressed with your broardmindedness and
disinterestedness.

Thanks to the Hiraoka Dam, which has been constructed with your great help
under the hard circumstances, and in the atmosphere of the bright world, now we
are able to have the opportunity to live here peacefully.

We hear that the authorities in our village promise you that they will record
your hardships and preciouness of peace, and that they will continue to pass down
this regrettable history from generation to generation, so as never to repeat that
awful war again.

In order to re-affirm it, they will write it down in a village history book
(The History of Tenryu Village) accurately, and they are also developing a plan
that they will build a memorial in memory of both the completion of the book and
your visiting here.

On the memorial they will carve the names of dozens of allied victims, who
lost their precious lives at Mitsusima in this foreign land and they will hold
a memorial service to comfort the spirits of the victims and to pray for the world
peace every year.

When it is completed in the future, of course we want to take part in this
memorial service.

We deeply appreciate the gentle feeling of your son Mr. Malcom rose and the
devoted act of Mrs. Keiko McNicoll, who is kind enough to show you over here.

~~Would you~~ please take care of yourself, Mr. William Rose. We hope for further
success in building " The Bridge of Peace " combined not only between England and
Japan but also among countries all over the world.

We also pray for your safe journey and having a wonderful time in Japan.

I want to conclude this welcome speech by expressing my appreciation for your
coming to Tenryu Village all the way in spite of your long journey.

Thank you very much indeed for coming, Mr. William Rose,

Transcript of the welcoming speech given by the head boy

129

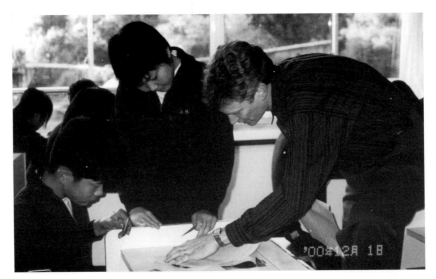

Children at the school in Mitsushima

Playground where the camp was situated

December 16th, 1999

Mr. William Rose

Are you fine? Thank you for the pretty handkerchief Has it snowed in your hometown yet? Here in Tenryu village we have a warm winter.

Thank you very much for the valuable experience at the exchange gathering on Dec. 11th. I have been in Tenryu village (for 14) years since I was born here. But I didn't know the past occurrences in this villa...

But I listened to...
your past valua...
answering my questi...
have a mind to... fo...
of your words in my f...
Christmas is coming soon...

Dear Mr. William Rose (③)

Thank you for coming to Tenryu village the other day.

I could know the history of Hiraoka which we had not known. And I feel I could learn how to live in my future life.

We collected the things we learned into some sheets of paper and put up them for the school festival held on December 23rd.

How do you like the hot spring, so-called "Okuyama no Yu"? Hot water was a little bit too hot for you wasn't it?

I often go there with my family. If I go there, I know about all of the people who work for that hot spring. I also know about all of the visitors who come here all the way from outside the prefecture.

So once I got the discount for the lunch charge by a woman who ...king a hot spring is very comfortable. And the ...

...Hiraoka this year yet So I wish it snows ...forward to the white Christmas.

...your name town yet?
...Christmas.

...for the pretty handkerchief.

Yours sincerely,
Nazuki Murasawa.

December 15, 1999

Dear Mr. William Rose (②)

Merry Christmas!

Thank you very much for your gift. Did it begin to snow in your home town? This year I'm very happy! In Tenryu village we have the mild Christmas unlike the usual year. I still sometimes think of you. I remember the warmth of your hand when I shook hands with you. I hope that we can meet again.

So I wish your health and Happy Christmas!

Yours sincerely,
Masahiro Toyama

December 16, 1999

...se (①)

...r cute handkerchief.
...carefully.
...that various things ...ad happened in Tenryu village.

For example, I didn't know about the history of Hiraoka Dam and the people who were take here to work for Hiraoka Dam.

I wish your healthfulness.

Good bye

Yours sincerely.

...Kisa Kawahara

Dear Mr. William...

Thank you for yo...
the war at the ex...
the other day.

I was not interested in the war very much, but we listened to your speech and could know how the war was. At the same time I began to think about the war.

Thank you very much for the wonderful experience at that day.

Yours sincerely, Kentaro Kumagai

Some of the letters from the children of the school in Mitsushima

The flag which we made in Japan coloured in with crayons

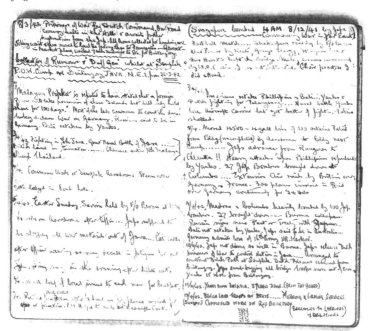

Actual pages from the original hand written wartime diaries, each page only 4" by 2" in size
(Both items above can be seen at The Imperial War Museum)

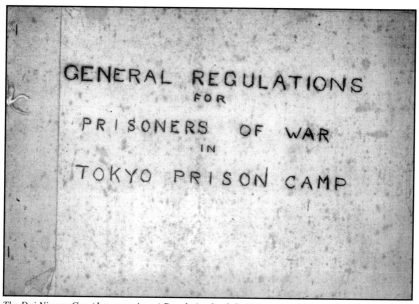

The Dai Nippon Gun (Japanese Army) Regulation book for Prisoners of War retained by W.C. Rose

2

be punished by the Nipponese Military Criminal Law or Military Disciplinary Law.
It is proper that if you attempt to escape from this camp or resist or disobey orders or commit improper acts you will be severely punished, furthermore guard soldiers might be forced to resort to the use of their rifles or bayonets.
Section 5- It is strictly prohibited amongst all prisoners to hold assemblies, give lectures, tell stories, hold parties or commit any kind of conspiracy regardless of how large or how small it may be.
Section 6- All prisoners should salute the Officer of the Day (N.C.O. of the Day) the same as you would salute your own superiors in your own army.
The salute for all Nipponese naval and military officers is the

Harsh discipline!

133

During our discussions, the village authorities indicated that preparations were being made to build a memorial to those allied prisoners who had died at the camp. This indeed happened with a dedication of the splendid memorial and elaborate ceremony near the school grounds on September 23rd 2000.

満島俘虜収容所
犠牲者慰霊碑建立除幕式

2000年9月23日（土）

長野県下伊那郡天龍村
満島俘虜収容所犠牲者慰霊実行委員会

Memorial dedication programme cover

Epilogue

My return visit, together with my eldest son Malcolm to Mitsushima near the village of Hiroaka has left me with an unforgettable feeling of warmth and reconciliation. The welcome was so rich and sincere from the village elders, the guests and from student representatives of the junior high school which is now on the site of the Prisoner of War Camp 1942-1945. The importance of the occasion is a lesson for the youth of today.

Looking around the assembled guests, there at the centre table was the family of Nishino San the one armed guard referred to in my book as the considerate and understanding guard (a good guy). It was a terrific gesture of good will which added a somewhat poignant note in as much as Nishino san had sadly died.

Nishino made it abundantly clear that he was in sympathy with our situation and he stood out clearly from others who were in charge of us. It was obviously apparent that his spiritual life was the reason for his attitude towards others.

In the period of 1942-45 it seemed a forlorn hope that we would ever be extradited from our trouble and live to tell the story. The thought of my ever returning to Japan was very far from my thinking as I flew out leaving behind the picture of the snow capped Mount Fuji, the last view of the land of my unexpected stay in unpleasant circumstances. Now in the year 2002 alongside me was Takako my son Graham's Japanese wife assisting me in the final proof checking of a story from my diaries making certain details were correct.

Truth is stranger than fiction, this is what reconciliation is all about.

AGAPE Ministries

Keiko Holmes O.B.E. was moved to begin her work of reconciliation between the Japanese people and their former enemies by the action of a small number of people in the rural district in which she was born. These relatively poor people built a garden of remembrance in honour of 16 British soldiers, Prisoners of War who had died while working in a local mine. By leading groups of FEPOWs and members of their families to visit this garden and to meet former Japanese soldiers, Keiko thought that some degree of reconciliation and peace of mind for those who had suffered might be achieved. This had proved to be the case. About 300 people have accompanied Keiko to Japan over the last 10 years, the work has spread to Holland, Canada, the USA, Australia, New Zealand and other countries in Asia.

Enquiries to:
Telephone: 020 7246 3918
www.agape-reconciliation.org
Email: keiko@agape-reconciliation.org

Forthcoming Publication

It is Proposed to produce a full historic technical reference book co-authored with Derek Peachey combining the original unabridged diaries in context with major ongoing events of the Second World War.

Enquiries to:
Tel/Fax: +44 (0) 1737-350698
Email: diary@gres.co.uk